Praise for Past Is Prologue

"Norman Levine embodies all of the virtues of what we call the "Trusted Advisor." What Norman knows and does will never go out of style. If more advisors had Norman's "way of being," advisor success and client loyalty would be way up and the need for compliance would be way down."

—Bill Bachrach, CSP
author of *Values-Based Financial Planning*

"Norman Levine has always been my personal hero. In this book, he shares many of the extraordinary techniques and skills that built this great industry and reveals how best to use them effectively in today's market place."

—*Robert C. Savage, CLU, ChFC*
Chairman of the Board, Savage & Associates, Inc.
Life and Qualifying Member of MDRT

"There is a crisis in financial services and Norman takes it head on in his eighth book. His sales ideas and timeless techniques can help anyone and everyone in this business."

—*Harry P. Hoopis, CLU, ChFC*
Managing Partner, Hoopis Financial Group, NMFN

"My dear friend Norman's new book for financial advisors remarkably captures the essence of yesterday's golden years, properly depicts the imperfections of the modern world, and provides an amazing road map for a wonderful and successful future."

—*Tom Wolff*, Industry legend and
author of *Sales Success, The Tom Wolff Way*

"Norman and I have been friends for many decades. We've traveled the same roads and experienced similar happenings. His new book should be utilized as a road map by modern day practitioners—and I highly recommend it."

O. Alfred Granum, CLU
Creator of the *One Card System* and
author of *Building a Life Insurance Clientlele*

"Thankfully, an industry Icon has once again drawn on his vast experience and shared his wisdom to illuminate our past as a definitive road map for the future."

Phillip C. Richards, CFP, CLU, RHU
Chairman of the Board, CEO
North Star Resource Group

"Norman Levine is one of the greatest in our field of insurance. I am proud to call him friend, my teacher and advisor. His vast knowledge shines through the pages of this book and he has a way to make it accessible and easy to understand by the reader. Not only has he written a great book again, but this one even surpasses his prior ones. The readers are in for a treat."

Mehdi Fakharzadeh
Author of *Nothing Is Impossible* and *Everything Is Possible*

For almost 60 years Norm Levine has been an astute observer and participant in the changing scene encompassing the life insurance business. Always ready to share his knowledge and experience, Norm again tells it like it was and is as well as how it ought to be."

Jack Bobo
Columnist, National Underwriter Life & Health/Financial Service
CEO and Executive Vice President, NALU (retired)

PAST IS PROLOGUE

Norman G. Levine, CLU, ChFC

Timeless Techniques
for Financial Advisors
in the 21st Century

Carter —
Best wishes for
success —
Norm G. Levine

ISBN 978-0-87218-961-4

Library of Congress Control Number: 2008922324

1st Edition

Printed in U. S. A.

About the Author

Norman Levine is one of the most applauded presenters, an internationally recognized speaker, trainer and consultant. He radiates the energy of success that has inspired over half a million people from groups of 10 to 15,000 throughout the U.S. and 23 countries to move beyond the ordinary into excellence in both their professional and personal lives.

Norman is a respected author and a giant in business with extraordinary corporate and entrepreneurial achievements in the areas of sales and management. His books, which have been translated into many languages and appeal to diverse industries, are: High Trust Leadership, Selling with Silk Gloves, Not Brass Knuckles; Yes You Can; How to Build a $100,000,000 Agency; From Life Insurance to Diversification; The Norman Levine Reader; and Passion For Compassion.

Through entertaining and informative customized presentations, Norman Levine will not only motivate you, but he will give you the tools and significant strategies for achieving new heights of accomplishments.

His primary areas of expertise are:

- Raising Sights and Expectations

- How to Reach Unrealized Potentials

- High Touch Sales Skills

- High Touch Management Skills

- Proven Time Management Methods

Norman's tried and true methods and processes are embraced by leaders in petroleum, high tech, manufacturing, automotive, apparel, hospitality, financial services and, of course, the insurance industry, where he is the only individual to have been honored with the life insurance industry's four highest levels of recognition. They are:

- Top of the Table – The Million Dollar Round Tables' highest level of sales success.

- Master Agency Award – The GAMA International's highest level of management success.

- Manager's Hall of Fame – The industry's top award, presented to one person each year for extraordinary achievement in management.

- John Newton Russell Memorial Award – The most prestigious of all as the yearly recipient is selected by industry wide blue ribbon committee from sales, management, academic, home office or field.

Norman thrives on effectively sharing his ideas and on creating "Winning Relationships". He and his wife, Sandy, have three children and five grandchildren. Norman and Sandy reside in Palm Springs, California.

Table of Contents

PART I
The Way It Was, The Way It Is,
The Way I Believe It Could and Should Be

PART II
Timeless Techniques and Concepts That Should be
Embraced by 21ST Century Financial Advisors

Foreword

Several good friends asked me to write this book on many different occasions, over a period of several years. Though I had written and published seven books previously, the theme of each of these new requests has been essentially the same and all suggested a subject I had never before addressed, except in social conversations. These friends were all aware of my expertise in the diversified financial service profession and my successful career as both a salesperson and manager (which had been the subjects of the earlier books), but they pointed out that I had also been blessed with longevity and was one of very few who could personally remember the way it was a long time ago, and what it's like now, and what valuable skills and techniques we have lost along the way.

Though reluctant to undertake a new book, and after years of procrastination, I have come to the conclusion that such a project would not only help the practitioner of today and tomorrow but would also preserve some wonderful times and fantastic memories of the last 60 years of the last century. Frankly, I got excited about sharing the best part of the good old days that the modern practitioner would benefit from by incorporating timeless techniques into their current practice.

As Shakespeare said — "The past is prologue," and I know the best financial advisors today do in fact incorporate the wisdom of the 20th century in their 21st century practice. I also know most contemporary advisors and all future candidates will only achieve their full potential by being exposed to the power of the true foundations of the profession of financial advising.

Hence this book. I believe it contains timeless treasures that will help all practitioners improve their productivity, make more money, have more fun, better serve their clients, their family, their community and their profession.

My Prologue

I thought sharing the personal story of my life, before and after I got into the serious business of providing financial products and services, might interest some readers. If you have no interest in how careers developed in the mid-20th century, skip this prologue and go right to Chapter One. On the other hand it might help you understand the way things were and how they evolved.

I have been in financial product sales and advising for over 60 years. Here is the story of how it came to be.

I graduated from high school, at the age of 16 in 1942. World War II was raging but my parents would not let me enlist until I turned 18. With almost two years to wait I started college at the University of Wisconsin majoring in my true loves, Ecology, Dairy Husbandry, and Ornithology. Campus life was great. Most males were off to war. It was not very crowded, and I was already quite knowledgeable in my chosen subjects. As a result, school work was easy and I had lots of time to hunt and fish. As an example of the situation, there was a wartime shortage of teachers so I was asked to teach Zoology II at the same time I was a student in Zoology I.

Time passed quickly, and as I approached my 18th birthday, I quit school and became an Army soldier within a month of turning 18. Off to Camp Croft in South Carolina, which was supposed to be for 16 weeks of basic training. After 8 weeks, in December of 1944, the Germans started a major counter-attack known as the Battle of the Bulge and the 106th Infantry Division was all but wiped out. They needed replacements quickly, so they aborted the 16-week program and I was off to Europe.

The convoy on the way over was horizon-to-horizon ships with us on troop carriers in the middle. Our speed was the speed of the slowest ship, and attacks by German submarines and our destroyers and corvettes dropping depth charges made for a slow crossing.

After two weeks of sailing, we anchored in Weymouth, England waiting for the Channel to be cleared so we could cross safely and get to France.

After two days, we finally ran the Channel and docked in France. For the next six months, we were in combat moving slowly towards Germany and the war's end.

I had purchased my first life insurance policy for $10,000 G.I. Insurance, which I still have in force today. Now the death benefit has grown to well over $30,000 and the cash value is almost $20,000.

Because I had been in active combat I was not relocated to the Pacific War Zone, as were many of the more recent arrivals, but remained in the Army of Occupation in Germany until 1946, when I was discharged and returned home.

As soon as possible I returned to a very crowded University of Wisconsin, which I found to be completely different. There was not enough housing, so myself and many others lived in barracks or Quonset huts, which had been used by the military during the war. We were miles away from the campus where all classes were over-filled.

I continued my chosen fields of education but it was very different. By the time my schooling was complete, I had matured enough to realize I was prepared for nothing practical.

Ecology was a word unknown to the masses. No one, not even the government, except in very rare circumstances, hired ecologists. I did not want to milk someone else's cows for the rest of my life, and I could never have afforded my own farm. Ornithology was, and still is, an expertise that was either a hobby or for academicians, which was not my strong suit. To further complicate the issue, I was not mentally prepared for a 9 to 5 disciplined workday and a five-day week.

The obvious conclusion was to go into business for myself and keep my natural history activities as a hobby. But at 21 years of age with no money to invest, what business could I enter?

I had an uncle who was what we would now call an independent multi-line insurance broker. He knew me well. I did not own a suit or tie. I had no money and no previous business experience, but he thought insurance was the career for me. He was a sole proprietor with no organization so he could only recommend the career and line me up with some companies, but otherwise I was on my own.

Reluctantly I took his advice. I moved back into my very supportive parents' home, and used the government provided veteran benefit, known as the G.I. Bill of Rights, to go to insurance classes and get my insurance licenses. Thanks to my uncle, the "Aetna Life and Casualty" (in those days a top-of-the-line Life and Property and Casualty company) opened an account for me, and I became an independent broker working out of my family home.

It was tough. I had no market, no training or natural sales skills, very superficial knowledge at best, and bills to pay. It was 1948 and thanks to my folks' generosity, including a rent-free home and office, borrowed money, and a few small sales, I survived until 1953. Though my first life insurance sale was in April 1948, I survived those first five years primarily on automobile and home-type insurance. Frankly, it was not working. It was a tough five years made even more difficult by marriage, a home of my own, and the arrival of a wonderful first child, a daughter, who is now also in our great business.

A client and neighbor was District Manager for a door-to-door brush and cleaning supply company "Fuller Brush." He suggested I take a territory; he would train me, and I would make a good living. Further, he suggested I could keep my insurance business on the side.

I was desperate, so I accepted. He taught me the products, how to display them, how to sell, and the necessary work ethic.

This was the first sales training and work discipline accountability I had ever been exposed to. This was my work schedule for the next two years. My insurance career was relegated to late night and weekends only. Fuller Brush was all day almost every day.

Up at 5:00 a.m.; out to my territory for that day where I put catalogues at each door (which I had to pay for) before 7:00 a.m. – over 100 each day. Then a quick cup of coffee and off to ring doorbells and retrieve my catalogs to use them again. When possible, if I could get past the door, I would do a sales pitch. No time for lunch, so I had a snack in my car. Kept going until dinner, which I had with my family, but then back out in the evening to try and see the people who were not home during the day. When sales were made I purchased the merchandise wholesale, and it was delivered to my home on Friday. Saturday, I delivered the merchandise and collected the retail price. I had to pay for my catalogs and the gift items I gave to each customer. Little things like scrub brushes or sample cologne.

This schedule meant I was working six days a week, 12 to 14 hours a day, paying for my supplies and attempting to see several hundred people per week. Rejection was a way of life and people skills were a necessity, which developed with practice.

It was fantastic preparation for a financial service career. After two years of Fuller Brush, in 1955 I figured out if I worked half as hard at insurance as I did at Fuller Brush, saw a fraction of the number of people, totally ignored rejection, and utilized the sales skills I had developed, insurance was a profession I could master.

In 1955 I resigned from Fuller Brush, arranged for some friends to take over my Property and Casualty insurance business, moved into an Aetna office, and became a full time life insurance agent. My business took off immediately and every year was better than the last. In 1953 and 1954 – while heavily into Fuller Brush – my name was not even on the Aetna leader list. In 1956 – my first full-time year as an agent – I was among the companies' top five producers. Fuller Brush really helped.

In 1959 Aetna asked me to start a new insurance agency, which I enthusiastically did and, within a few years, grew it to the biggest life insurance agency in the company – we won the Aetna's President's Trophy for over 10 consecutive years.

During those years I became heavily involved in industry organizations and, in time, became the National Association of Life Underwriters (NALU – now NAIFA) President of the New York City, the New York State, and the National Associations.

I was also active in the General Agents and Managers Association (GAMA), serving as the New York City, the San Francisco, and the National President.

The Life Underwriters Training Council (LUTC) was where it all began. I started as New York City Chairman in 1955 and eventually became National Chairman.

As a qualifying member of the Million Dollar Round Table, and an occasional Top-of-the-Table qualifier, and a more frequent Court of the Table qualifier, I also held many positions in MDRT, including Regional Vice President.

There was much more in the involvement area, in and outside our industry, which resulted in many awards, but among the most prestigious are the GAMA. Master Agency award, its Hall of Fame Designation, and the most prestigious of all, the industry's John Newton Russell Memorial Award. In the educational area I studied for and received the CLU (Chartered Life Underwriters), ChFC (Chartered Financial Consultant), and RFC (Registered Financial Consultant) designations.

During all those years I have received far more than I have given in every endeavor. What I have learned, and the friends I have made, are the priceless treasures that make life worthwhile.

Let us now skip ahead to the early 70's when I left the Aetna and, using my accumulated experience (much of which is included in the upcoming chapters of this book), built the "Levine Financial Group," a pioneer in full service financial advising.

However, before I left the Aetna in the mid 60's, the company had required all agency managers to take the SEC Series One examination and become Broker Dealers for investments. We were not registered representatives but actual Broker Dealers. The Aetna had bought PALIC (the Participating Annuity Life Insurance Company), which was a pioneer in the Variable Life and Annuity field and very controversial at the time. Up until then the Aetna and most other life insurance companies would not allow their representatives to be registered representatives and sell investment products. This was the very beginning of what is now called convergence.

I didn't like the variable products we were required to sell because I was indoctrinated in selling conservative guaranteed products. In contrast, PALIC's products were not guaranteed, were grossly overpriced, and paid unreasonably high commissions. Therefore, my agency associates and I sold very few variable products.

However, this experience opened my eyes to a new world. The Financial Advisor's mission was to provide our clients with security against the three greatest risks all people face: Living too long – dying too soon – and the hazards they face along the way. We claimed to do that with a very limited insurance-only portfolio, but I knew we weren't doing a complete job. Although I was the head of Aetna's leading life insurance agency, I resigned to create a truly full financial service operation capable of really providing total financial security for our clients.

Since I respected my 27 year relationship with the Aetna, I did not want to steal the agency I had built from scratch and have my agent associates come with me, so I decided a personal major geographic move was necessary. I left New York City where my agency was housed and moved to San Francisco to begin all over again.

I reasoned that to do a complete financial advising service for our clientele, we needed a completely diversified financial service company. I further decided I could not, nor could any other individual, be an expert in all the different products and services, so we had to have specialist experts available for me and my associate advisors to utilize to best serve our clients. This was truly revolutionary, and as it turned out, prophetic for the entire financial service industry.

By the mid-70's, headquartered in San Francisco, California, the Levine Financial Group, with 11 sub offices spread from Fairbanks, Alaska in the north to Fresno, California in the south, was pioneering the financial advising concept. In our headquarters we had six corporations, one for a primary life insurance company, one for multiple brokerage life insurance companies, one for property and casualty insurance, one for pensions, one for other employee benefits, and one for fee-based financial advising. We also had an unincorporated investment company and housed two rent-paying attorneys and one rent-paying accountant. They maintained their own private practices but were available for free consultations with our advisors to discuss client situations.

The Levine Financial Group quickly became one of the largest financial service organizations in the world and the concepts we pioneered and paid to create have since been the model for many modern-day organizations.

After over 50 years of proudly being part of an industry I love, once again it was time for a change. I had built two large organizations, one in the East and one in the West, been a significant personal producer, been an industry activist, written and had published seven books, raised a family of three great children, all of whom chose to become financial service practitioners, and enjoyed a whole life partnership with my fantastic loving wife. My concern for the industry's future suggested that I spend the past 10 years and whatever additional time I will be allowed, to in effect, pass the baton to the next generation. As a speaker, writer, consultant, and coach, I am very aware that much of what I, and my peers from my generation, know is essential for great success today. Unfortunately, much of these treasures either has been forgotten or was lost in transmission because of the distractions of change.

Company training programs, visible heroes, and a sharing and caring culture have all been greatly neglected because of compliance, cost control, technical procedures, and a *'what's in it for me'* attitude.

The rest of this book, after an overview of from whence we came, where we are, and where we may be going, will be dedicated to sharing timeless concepts, skills, techniques, and ideas that can and should be utilized to make the reader's career, and the broad financial service industry, achieve it's fantastic potential.

Chapter 1

THE WAY IT WAS

Before I attempt to share my perception of "The way it was," I would like to define the time frame about which we will reminisce.

Let me start by sharing with you a letter I received from a friend of over 50 years, Tom Wolff (an industry legend). On the occasion of my birthday he sent a beautiful letter sharing many thoughts. One in particular was a reference back to the *"Golden Years."* He suggested that the last century, particularly in the 50's, 60's and 70's, he had always remembered as the Golden Years. They were the most fun and had the greatest impact on his and my development.

He mentioned that it was interesting that his children, as well as my children, both followed us into the financial service business. And regrettably, will never know the wonders of those magic, Golden Years.

He went on to suggest that perhaps that's a good thing because if they knew what he and I remember they might not enjoy their current careers as much as they all do.

All that notwithstanding, though I completely understand and agree with Tom, I will share in this chapter much of what I remember of how the business was, then in the next chapter, discuss the way it now is, and in the following chapter, though many changes are for the better, I will share some of the great pleasures and techniques of the Golden Years that have been lost along the way. For example, we have lost some of the excitement and motivation, along with skills and techniques, which if relearned and implemented in today's world would certainly contribute to a more fulfilling career experience. They would also surely improve advisor productivity, while also better serving the client, and incidentally the advisor would also be having more fun.

Those Golden Years cannot be identified with a snapshot of any one particular year. My observations will include, from personal experience, the 40's, 50's, 60's and part of the 70's, but will also include the pre-World War II era as it was described to me by my early mentors and heroes.

Actually from the turn of the 20th century and well into the 60's the financial service business changed very little. It was essentially much the same until the late 60's when slowly change began to impact the industry, and then with an accelerating pace in the 70's and 80's, the new world was born. By the 90's and the start of the 21st century, it was in some ways a different industry.

Let me also share a disclaimer of sorts, since I came into the business as an insurance salesman who did both Property and Casualty and Life Insurance business concurrently for the first seven years of my career and then became a full-time, exclusive Life Insurance agent in 1955. My initial impressions were through the eyes of an insurance salesperson. Therefore, though I will try to be objective about all the different components that today make up the financial service business, there might be some slightly distorted perspectives because of my own personal career experience. However, I am convinced the overview is essentially correct.

In those early years, financial services were in fact a group of super specializations with each segment exclusively representing its own product lines. Though we practiced our own particular specialties, we were exposed in competition to the other specialties but, in most instances, were only licensed to sell our specific products.

> In those early years, financial services were in fact a group of super specializations with each segment exclusively representing its own product lines.

Beginning with the banking industry is a perfect example. Banks and savings banks were classically housed in very impressive structures with multiple customer windows, often with bars separating the teller (bank clerk) from the customer, and all business was transacted through those windows and at arms length. Basically, all the banks did was take, hold, and secure money. They had Trust Departments that targeted the very wealthy and for all intents and purposes no other products.

Savings banks in New York and Massachusetts were allowed to manufacture and distribute savings bank life insurance but with very severe limitations. The amount of insurance, the variety of insurance, and their allowable markets were restricted by regulation. Some insurance industry activists were concerned with banks becoming far more aggressive in the insurance field and the limits being significantly expanded. But that never happened.

The market for the professional proactive life insurance agent rarely conflicted with the relatively weak marketing expertise of a bank representative. As a matter of fact, having a little savings bank life insurance helped build the foundation of a portfolio upon which a qualified life insurance agent could superimpose a significantly more comprehensive and larger overall plan. I never personally felt the banks were a threat, and if anything, they helped me develop credibility and larger sales with my clientele. It is interesting that many life insurance activists were concerned with the development of financial products by any institution, other than a traditional life insurance company, even the Federal Government.

For example, when Social Security came into being some life insurance prophets of doom predicted that would be the end of the insurance industry. In actual practice, it was the catalyst that significantly expanded the life insurance segment of the financial service community and upon which large and significant financial plans were eventually superimposed. Social Security was a catalyst in educating the public to their own financial responsibility and it prepared a foundation upon which total financial plans could be built. So both banks and the Government, with their very specific and limited product lines, had a very positive effect on the development of life insurance careers.

However, banks were aware of the potential profit in other financial sales opportunities so they did try, through changes in regulation and legislation, to expand their portfolio of products. In broad terms, and for several decades they were generally, relatively ineffective.

I attended a meeting of bankers during the year when things were just beginning to change, and one of them reported that they had set up a desk in their banking facility for, in effect, comprehensive financial advising including insurance products, and the bank reported that the question their financial advisor specialist was asked most frequently was "Where is the restroom?"

Also, the government was somewhat concerned with the information banks had accumulated on their depositors. There was a fear that they were in position, theoretically, to pressure their account holders who were interested in borrowing money or getting a better rate of interest, to do other than banking business with the bank in order to benefit from some very favorable banking deals. As a result, the banks were restrained by regulation and legislation from aggressively diversifying during a good part of the last century. Besides the regulatory limitations however, bank executives and most certainly bank tellers, were unskilled and uneducated to be successful proactive financial advisors. In my opinion they never, in the 20th century, developed as significant competitors to the rest of the financial service world, but did a very good job in expanding and improving banking services.

Real estate salespeople were few and far between and mortgage brokers were non-existent. Prior to World War II, real estate brokers handled home or commercial sales and usually had direct arrangements with banks or lending institutions for financing. There was a tremendous change after World War II with millions of G.I.'s coming back from overseas service, getting married and having children, which resulted in the so-called baby-boomer generation. Housing was at a premium. Builders all over the country began tract-type housing at remarkably low cost.

The classic example in the 40's was a builder by the name of Levitt. He built, in the suburban area of New York City, what was then known as Levittown. The houses in Levittown were quite comfortable with at least two bedrooms and a small piece of land. The houses all looked alike but, they were available for as little as $7,500 a house. This was an extraordinary development, I believe, involving thousands of homes. At the same time smaller tract housing developments were popping up coast to coast. My first stand-alone home cost approximately $12,000 and was one of 35 houses also in a suburban area of New York City. This was perceived by my friends as an upscale home. I had three bedrooms and two baths on a 60' by 100' lot with a backyard area, which I gardened, and a neat little front lawn. It had an attached garage, and although there were several models in our development to choose from, they were not very different than thousands and thousands of similar homes all over the United States.

The developers marketed the houses themselves and arranged for mortgages directly with pre-arranged lenders. As I said, at that time, independent real estate salesmen were very unusual and there were no mortgage brokers soliciting mortgage loans. Since the houses in these communities were usually purchased by returning veterans, recently married, and just starting families, each community was also the hub of the social life of friends and neighbors all experiencing a new lifestyle at the same time. Sharing and caring was the name of the game. You borrowed things from your neighbors. The wives, most of whom were not yet working, would get together for coffee klatches during the day while the men went off to work and the babies grew up in a very happy, sharing environment. Since these homes were all in suburbia, everyone had at least one car and the values and traditions of our parents and grandparents were maintained and perpetuated.

All those houses appreciated along with the inflationary impact on the entire economy, and as the returning veterans improved their economic position, they either significantly upgraded their homes or sold their first home and used it as the deposit for a more impressive second home. By then, real estate agents were becoming visible but the environment stayed pretty constant until the 60's. The children of the Baby-Boomers began to kick up their heels, perhaps because of the Vietnam War, perhaps as a protest against society. Sharing and caring was replaced by *"What's in it for me?"* and anti-establishment and anti-government movements began to proliferate among the younger generation. Drugs became much more available and abused and the traditions of marriage were being substantially moderated.

Though at first blush it might seem out of context to discuss this part of society in a chapter dedicated to the 'way it was' in the financial service business, there is no question that as society changed it had a tremendous impact on all of the financial institutions. As you will read in the next chapter, similar type changes were occurring in the varied financial institutions.

During those Golden Years, the investment business was relatively straightforward. It was primarily built on stocks and bonds purchased through stock brokers. My first job after graduating from high school, beginning college, and waiting to enter the military service in World War II, was with a stock brokerage firm, H. Hentz & Co., in the financial district in New York City. I was a boardroom runner. The salary was $14 a week; which really wasn't bad for the time. World War

During those Golden Years, the investment business was relatively straightforward.

II was already on and employers looking for older employees found it very limited so they took anyone they could get, even a young inexperienced person like myself.

The Boardroom consisted of rows of desks facing a projected-stock ticker tape and at each desk a stockbroker sat with a telephone. There were no computers. My job was when they wanted a price quote, they would give me a slip of paper, and I ran it back to the cage where they then found out the current price, wrote it on a slip of paper, and I delivered it back to the broker. If a sale was consummated over the telephone, which was the way almost all the sales were in fact negotiated, I again took the order form on a piece of paper to the cage, and when the sale was completed, brought it back to the stockbroker.

Basically the only products the stockbrokers were selling were stocks and bonds. Just as it was in banking and real estate, stockbrokers were specialists. Mutual funds had not yet been developed, and all of the various other investment vehicles were not yet part of their portfolio. Little did I know, in a way, that was the beginning of my financial service career and I one day would be a broker doing the same kind of thing as part of a totally diversified portfolio.

Another glaring difference in that era was that almost all people in the financial service profession, whether in insurance, investments, or real estate, were men. Most women were not yet working, although many did during World War II to help with the war effort, but in the so-called professions, men represented almost 100% of the participants. There were some minor changes in that area in the 50's and 60's but it wasn't until the late 60's and 70's that real attention was given to women entering all of the professions. Along with many other innovations, I was one of the pioneers of that movement. I began to train and develop women in the early 60's and helped form an organization that was know as the National Association of Female Executives (N.A.F.E.), whose President, Wendy Rue, helped me recruit female sales representatives. I was one of the few male members, and eventually became Vice President. By then my insurance organization had a significant number of women representatives.

The Property and Casualty insurance business was also highly specialized during those Golden Years. Not only was the business specialized, but the product lines were as well. There were no homeowner policies, so you had to sell a separate fire insurance policy for the risks of fire and another one for burglary and another one for liability, and the automobile policy was also separated into different segments. With so many returning veterans buying homes and cars for the first time, it was significantly easier to sell Property and Casualty insurance for specific needs than it was to create life insurance sales. As a result, most Property and Casualty agents sold little or no life insurance. It required a different skill, and again, they were comfortable as super-specialists. The true multi-line company had not yet fully developed, and even when they did come into being, the individual representatives for most of the 20th century were far more at ease with Property and Casualty type sales than with Life Insurance or Investment sales. As a result, even within the insurance profession, Property and Casualty and Life Insurance were in effect separate and very specialized, though many sales representatives were licensed for both.

When I decided, after my Fuller Brush experience, to become a Life Insurance agent I did what almost everyone else in the business had done. I chose to specialize and turned my Property and Casualty business over to a friend. We had an alliance of sorts where he referred his Life Insurance prospects to me and I referred my Property and Casualty clients to him. Eventually, when I created the Levine Financial Group, a fully diversified financial service company, in the early 70's, I built a Property and Casualty company into my organization so we could fully serve our clientele.

The Life Insurance specialty will now be addressed in the rest of this chapter. The introduction of Social Security and Savings Bank Life Insurance notwithstanding, the public perception of Life Insurance agents pre- and post- World War II was pretty low on the ladder of prestige and professionalism. There were hundreds of thousands of Life Insurance agents all over the country aggressively pushing the sale of the product and not really solving clients' needs and wants. Though I knew the situation, I also knew that it was a correct fit for me. I wanted to be in business for myself and didn't have the wherewithal to start any other kind of business, but the decision was not well-received by my good friends and relatives.

My dad was the most influential person in my life as a supporter, mentor, and role model, and had always supported anything I chose to do. He was a doctor, a professional man with very high standards; but whatever I chose to pursue he encouraged me without qualification. By finishing high school at a young age, serving in World War II, going to university with people much older than I was, who thought I was their age, along with the opportunity to be away from home, all resulted in my getting into all kinds of unusual things. In retrospect, I now realize my dad didn't support and admire many of my youthful experiments, nonetheless, no matter what I chose to do, dad would always say, 'Norman, if that's what you want to do, go ahead and do it, only be the best you can be." Those experiments included farming, boxing, bar tending, selling, and lots more. Each time dad was totally supportive.

When I finally told him that I had decided to become an insurance person he again was supportive but with a different message. This is close to word for word, since I've never forgotten it. He said, "Son, if that's what you want to do, go ahead and do it. Just remember, I want you to be the best you can be. And I don't want you to worry, because if you get married and have children, I'll see to it that financially they have a good upbringing, and I'll see to it that they get a good education. So you just go ahead and be an insurance man if that's what you really want to be."

I knew where he was coming from because most people in the insurance business were not doing that well and they didn't have a very good reputation. However I knew there were some that were extraordinary and that it was the beginning of a very promising profession, and I believed I could survive and prosper.

Before I go on with insurance in the Golden Years, let me tell you that my dad watched me develop and was fully aware of my success and progress, but he was not a hugger, he was a hand-shaker, and he rarely verbalized love and affection, though I was always aware of its presence. So he never said anything about my success in my new chosen career. And then one day, the inevitable happened and he had a severe heart attack. I went to visit him in the intensive care ward of the hospital, and with oxygen in his nose and the beeper of the machine beeping behind him, he took my hand, and he said, "Norman, if I had my life to live over again, instead of being a physician, I'd want to be an insurance man just like you." I cried then and I am almost crying as I write these words. That was the greatest gift my dad ever gave me and he gave me lots of them.

But I tell that story here because it will give you an idea of how the insurance profession developed and matured during those wonderful Golden Years. We went from peddlers pushing products to professionals making the world a better place. We did it by caring and sharing, not just for our client, but for our peers. There was no competition. Everyone freely shared and helped their fellow practitioner develop into the kind of professional we all aspired to be.

There were well over one hundred traditional life insurance companies in those days, primarily marketing through a career agency system. They recruited agents aggressively and paid salaries or draws to get them started. Most companies had training programs of one kind or another, sometimes in the home offices, sometimes at the field level. In 1948 when I joined The Aetna, I was a Multiple-line Agent doing more Property and Casualty than Life, but in 1955 I became a full-time career agent with The Aetna. They sent me to Hartford for a three-week school, but I had significant work to do before I was allowed to attend. Once I got to the school, I was tested for a word-for-word sales presentation and if I hadn't had it down to the punctuation marks I would have been sent home. It was an intense few weeks with full day classes, evening homework, and lots of role play. Though the school was run by a professional training director, the teachers were primarily successful salespeople who aspired to management and, in transition, were used to teach the schools.

> There were well over one hundred traditional life insurance companies in those days, primarily marketing through a career agency system.

This was one of the better training programs, but all companies had something like The Aetna plan to get folks off to a fast start. The agency that recruited you was classically in nice office space, in a Class A building, with quality furniture, and for those days, all of the technical support you could hope for. There were no computers so there were hand-cranked adding machines and calculators on some of the desks, telephones, and we were each given a rate book which was hard-bound, since nothing ever changed, and we could use it until it wore out. Some of the greatest producers of that era literally memorized a good part of those rate books right down to the penny. There were a limited number of policies available, and since it was the only product line in our portfolio, it was used for every conceivable need, including death, emergency cash, retirement, disability or whatever. So-called need selling had not yet come into favor. I will discuss the evolution of selling later in this book but for now I will just share the basic and primitive techniques of the last century.

Most life insurance was either sold by full-time career life insurance agents, who represented what were described as career agency traditional legal reserve life insurance companies, or by debit agents, representing industrial-type insurance companies. Some of the better known industrial companies were Metropolitan, Prudential, and John Hancock, all of which did both career and industrial type distribution.

The traditional agents did essentially what agents and brokers do today but the debit agent had a completely different system. Both sales groups, in the early and mid-20th century, used sales techniques that were the lowest level of product pushing.

The debit agents were given a geographic territory that was just large enough to call on every household in a stipulated time frame, perhaps every week or every month. They would ring every door bell but had to call on every company policyholder in their territory on a scheduled basis. They each had a debit "Book" for which they were responsible. Their primary product was life insurance, usually for very small amounts, and for which premiums were by the week rather than the year. Premiums were often as little as dimes and quarters per visit. Unlike the traditional agent, the debit agent actually collected the premium on their scheduled visits. Of course they also had the second job of trying to sell new or additional insurance to the companies' existing clients and to anyone else they could reach in their debit territory. Occasionally, they would be able to make a somewhat larger sale.

Therefore, though the debit agent collected premiums and could sell very small weekly premium products and the traditional agent did not, they both were trying to sell new life insurance as a primary job function. In the first half of the 20th century, professional skills were not yet developed though a few practitioners had self-educated to higher standards.

Most debit and traditional agents traded on scare tactics and gimmicks. Pre-war and into the 40's and 50's, some agents I knew carried a miniature coffin in their attaché case and placed it in front of prospects and told them some day they would die.

Others carried a toy that would take in blank paper and when cranked, put out dollar bills. The point is they traded on fear and death and verbally backed up the hearse. Of course they would offer life insurance and attempt to make a sale.

This of course is a description of many life insurance peddlers but a more professional type was beginning to develop.

No wonder my dad was less than enthusiastic about a life insurance career. As a physician he had been a target for many aggressive insurance salespeople.

This was the beginning. Post-World War II saw the industry moving towards upgrading and professionalism. Education and training along with ethical and modern standards eliminated the bad and created a new and wonderful profession.

Another challenge of the times was life insurance premiums. By today's standards, they were embarrassingly high and term insurance was perceived as a product of last resort and generally considered a *no-no*. Term insurance was several times as expensive as it is now, and it didn't have any cash accumulation so that it served a single purpose – dying too soon, or some day being converted to a permanent plan.

Most companies' rates were pretty much the same. There were a few companies that were stock companies and they did not generally pay dividends on their policies. The initial premium appeared cheaper since the policyholder was not a part owner of the company and received no dividends.

Most of the better companies were mutual companies owned by the policyholders, and though the premiums might have been slightly higher initially, the dividends made up the difference in a hurry. Over the long haul, the accumulation of the cash value and dividends substantially exceeded the return of a non-participating policy.

The chief executives of the companies were paid a reasonable salary, but in almost every company the better producers made more money than the President or the Chairman. The successful agent was perceived to be the most valuable person in the company and everyone on the company payroll was dedicated to supporting the agent and the agency system. The agents freely shared sales ideas and concepts and not only worked together, they played together.

By now the reader might get the impression the Golden Years may not have been all that golden. There has never been a time, and there never will, when everything is perfect. There is always some good and always some bad. The Golden Years for insurance that I allude to were not perfect but they were wonderful years for the "Practitioner."

The environment we lived in, now often referred to as Karma, was truly extraordinary. It existed year-round in every company and in every professional organization. I could write chapters on this one subject but let me use just one example to illustrate the point, "company incentive-based conventions."

First to fully feel and understand the impact of the times, you must know the lifestyle of the average person in most of the last century. Most people never flew on an airplane and rarely traveled beyond short distances from home. Cars and trains were the most frequent means of transportation. Most people only were aware of how the rich and famous lived because of the movies, as there was no television and the great, great majority had never seen it first hand.

When a recruit entered our industry, myself included, they were often only in their 20's (I was 21) and at best of moderate means.

Their general agent or manager was living in what they perceived to be a mansion, belonged to a fancy club, traveled to exotic places, and enjoyed a community and professional position of great respect.

The top agent producers had all of the same and both managers and agent were treated as celebrities by the company home office.

This image was what often attracted the recruit into the business and then motivated him (there were few if any women recruits) to work hard and succeed.

The example of company conventions, which only happened for a few days once a year, is not out of context because the attitude I am about to describe was year-round.

Qualification for a convention was a worthy goal but reasonably attainable and modest. The convention site was a very upscale resort that was recognized for its elite clientele and usually had golf, tennis, horseback riding, skeet shooting, etc. It was probably in an exotic location most agents had only dreamed about.

All expenses, including travel, were paid for by the company and spouses and children were welcome. Often, for additional production requirements, some of the family's expenses were also paid.

All of the company super-producers, as well as the first year struggling qualifiers, attended the same meeting and social visits and brain picking sharing was always automatic and presumed.

When the qualifier arrived at the entrance to this fantastic place, an entourage was there to greet him. This always included the Senior Vice Presidents, Vice Presidents, Superintendents and Director of Agencies and sometimes the President and CEO of the company. Even if it was the qualifiers first meeting, somehow, almost miraculously, the entire entourage greeted him and his spouse with a first name greeting.

Though rooms were assigned with the biggest producers and largest agency heads getting suites, all the rooms were superior to anything the typical agent had ever enjoyed before.

If there weren't enough quality rooms to go around, except for the very top officers, the bad rooms were given to the Home Office people. The agent was "King."

The upscale hotel dress code was mandated and at least one dinner was black tie. The "educational meetings" were conducted and completed by lunch time and for the rest of the day there were poorly attended workshops because they conflicted with golf and tennis tournaments or pool side pleasures.

There were cocktail parties before every dinner and usually dancing after dinner, and occasionally midnight buffets, often pool side.

Agencies within the company, with large qualifying delegations, usually hosted one or two private parties somewhere along the line for just their own people.

The key to this overview is everyone was loyal to their company, the company was dedicated to and loyal to their producers, and every agent looked forward to, and attended, every meeting.

Can you imagine a 21-year-old first-year agent qualifying and being flown with his family, perhaps to the Greenbriar, and entering a world they had never seen before?

As I suggested, this is just one example of year-round care and attention for agents that was enjoyed for most of the 20th century.

Some of the same existed on an inter-company and industry environmental basis. For example the National Association of Life Underwriters (NALU) was building to a membership of 140,000 where representatives of every company and all the agencies worked together, played together, and shared with each other. The whole industry was committed to a common cause.

Direct mail and telephone solicitation was built into the training of every agent because agents were expected to see 15 people a week as a minimum and to make some sales every week. Obviously, many didn't reach those goals, but that was the target and that was what was aggressively promoted by management and accountability was part of the relationship. As a great role model, Johnny Utz, a great industry activist, set a record of selling at least one policy a day for several decades.

The most illustrious production organization was The Million Dollar Round Table. In 1927, 32 agents, each of whom sold over one million dollars of life insurance a year (a tremendous achievement in those days), met at the Peabody Hotel in Tennessee and created MDRT. The organization reached full speed after World War II, and initially qualification was based only on sales volume. If you did a million dollars of insurance, you could be a member. It was a very prestigious organization even though a very small percentage of the people in the industry achieved the Million Dollar Round Table target. The membership during the Golden Years was primarily from the United States and secondarily Canada.

> The most illustrious production organization was The Million Dollar Round Table.

The meetings were motivational and inspirational, and the speakers were all practitioners or people dedicated to the well-being of practitioners, and there to share all they knew. There were few, if any, speakers who were entertainers or people who made a profession of speaking and were paid for their services.

The biggest producers were heroes and mentors and very visible. Both at NALU meetings and MDRT meetings you would see the superstars in the lobbies sharing freely with crowds of aspiring young people, who were "picking their brains" and enjoying the personal contact with their heroes. The profession was almost a religion, with everyone committed to the common cause.

However, the Life Insurance product line was pretty feeble. Not only were the premiums significantly higher than they are today, the variety of products consisted basically of three different primary policies: Term Insurance, Whole Life, or a variety of it, with limited payment provisions, and Endowments, with a small variety of forms.

One of the Endowment policies was called the Life Income Policy. It matured with a face amount that generated, when converted to settlement options at the rate of $10 per month for each $1,000 of face amount, for life. So if someone wanted a retirement benefit of $100 a month for life, they'd buy a $10,000 Life Income policy. It was more expensive than a regular Endowment but only because you had to accumulate more cash value by retirement age.

Initially, as I suggested, the rate books were hard bound because there were few changes until the 60's. There were some marketing variations that were very interesting. There were a series of policies called Family Income or Family Maintenance policies where the death benefit was calculated to provide $10 of income for each $1,000 of face amount for different periods of time. It was actually a combination of Whole Life and decreasing Term Rider. Also, there was the Jumping Juvenile contract, a policy intended for children that started at a lesser amount and at some point in the future increased five-fold – so if you bought a $5,000 policy on a young child, at age 20, if that was the calculated transition date, it became a $25,000 policy.

There were also family plans where you could buy a policy on the breadwinner and automatically get a small amount of insurance on each of the children and the spouse. These innovations required that the rate book allow for flexibility and most companies switched to loose-leaf binders instead of hard-cover, fixed rate books. Still the variety of choices was very limited.

Despite these minor changes, as I already said, the premium rates from company to company were essentially the same. I can remember one instance when I didn't have the rate book of the company I intended to sell, but I did have the rate book of a competing company, and I quoted the other company's rate, telling the client it wasn't the exact rate, but rather an approximation. The difference, and it was only for a $10,000 policy, was less than a dollar when the policy was actually issued.

This limited variety of policy forms resulted in life insurance agents, who in effect had only life insurance in their portfolio, to implement plans (using only life insurance) for retirement for those who lived "too long" and cash and income-producing plans if they "died too soon" and some cash accumulation for "emergencies." Since very little term insurance was sold, life insurance almost always provided some cash equity. There were even some policies that allowed for a disability income rider if the insured became disabled. The bottom line was the solution for dying too soon, living too long, or becoming disabled along the way was always life insurance. Of course at the same time, the investment practitioners, who in time included mutual funds, were making the same claims for their limited investment portfolio.

Since there were no computers and we didn't have the capacity to design so-called advanced plans in the office, we would calculate the premium on our own hand-cranked calculator, and the company provided standard forms for us to use. Plans that were perceived to be advanced underwriting, such as business continuity, retirement plans, estate tax situations, etc., were sold by filling in the blanks on otherwise standard completed forms for sales presentations. The forms were prepared by the legal department of the companies, and they were provided for the sales force who only had to fill in the blank spaces with the calculated premiums.

In retrospect it was a very simple world. In time we learned we had been charging too much for too little, but everyone who bought the insurance was taking a positive step towards increased financial security and were better off for doing so. When premiums were reduced the consumer was even better for it.

The specialization concept was so strong that life insurance companies into the 60's and 70's would not allow their sales representatives to get registered to sell any equity products. As a matter of fact, if anyone did try to sell a variable or an equity product, in many cases they'd be terminated by the insurance company.

Mutual funds showed up during this era and they developed a plan where you could pay on a scheduled basis, which was in effect dollar-cost averaging. In each month, or whatever schedule they chose, whatever the regular investment and the current cost of the funds would determine how many shares your deposit would buy. Mutual Funds salesmen went directly head-to-head with Life Insurance agents claiming that Mutual Funds did everything Life Insurance could do and would build a better equity base in a shorter period of time. Some of them even began to sell Mutual Funds along with some inexpensive Term Insurance so they had both a death benefit and a wealth accumulation vehicle. The loads on these Mutual Funds contractual dollar cost-averaging plans were quite high as were the commissions, and eventually they were withdrawn from the marketplace.

When we reached the 60's there were some small changes beginning in every aspect of the financial service industry, but almost everyone was still specializing in their own product lines; however, one could sense that bigger changes were coming.

In 1939 at the New York World's Fair, I saw my first television set. It was just a few inches across and black and white and very blurry. It was very exciting and I couldn't wait until I could buy one for myself. Computers were not yet even considered. Along came World War II and all progress in those areas was halted with the country making a total commitment to winning the war. When the war ended, we began to hear about computers, television, and new communication vehicles. It was predicted that these would take over the financial service world and everything else in our society within five or 10 years. It has now happened, but it took a lot longer than was predicted.

In that regard, insurance companies that were burdened with lots of employees, high overhead, and all kinds of paperwork, began to embrace computerization in the early days of the technology.

In the 70's I arranged to have a room in my agency dedicated to computers, which required climate control and a sealed environment. We literally filled the room with computer equipment that worked on a card system instead of disks and memory and began to see the value of computerization. However, by today's standards it was so primitive it was almost ridiculous. That entire room didn't generate as much power, nor as much memory, nor was it nearly as efficient as a laptop computer is today. By the 70's, and certainly in the 80's, change was on the way and the beginnings were already here.

In the insurance industry from an educational point of view, besides necessary skill training, before World War II, "The American College" was promoting the Chartered Life Underwriter designation: "CLU" At first relatively few people actually qualified until after the war and then it became a mission for most people in our industry. By the 60's a significant number of life agents were enrolled in the CLU study program and in time, usually within five years, they'd get their CLU designation, which they'd use after their name. The classes were given with required live attendance and exams were given twice a year in designated examination sites with a proctor present.

The Life Underwriter Training Council (LUTC) had been initiated prior to World War II and it was created by LIAMA, the Life Insurance Agency Marketing Association, which is now called LIMRA – the Life Insurance Marketing and Research Association, and NALU, the National Association of Life Underwriters, now known as NAIFA – the National Association of Insurance and Financial Advisors. When World War II came along it was put on hold and didn't get aggressively promoted until after the war ended. LUTC students got some basic education, but the best skills training available anywhere. This was another step towards increasing the professional image of the industry.

Those were fun days. Lots of good things were happening and we were learning how to inter-relate with people, see lots of people, and help our prospects and clients achieve solutions to their financial problems, even though we were limited by our portfolio of products.

Most life insurance companies were doing extremely well. The profit margins on the products that we had were substantial and so the companies provided lots of support, training programs, social opportunities, generous pension plans, and lots, lots more.

At that stage, brokerage business was rare. Almost all the business was being generated by full-time career representatives. Several companies did solicit brokerage but their target market was mostly Property and Casualty agents, who incidentally sold some, but relatively little, life insurance.

Then another change began that heavily impacted the financial service industry. As the different financial specializations began to look for ways to expand their portfolio into areas previously the private domain of their competitors, several things began to happen. Every specialty looked to diversify their product portfolio into areas never before considered. For example, Universal Life, which is today a universally marketed life insurance product, was conceived by a stock brokerage firm. For the first time we had a life insurance product with variables built into the premium and the benefits. Also, price competition and increased brokerage production began to force down the premiums on all forms of insurance with the most dramatic impact being on term insurance. Term insurance rates fell to a fraction of what they had been. Traditional old line companies initially said it was impossible to issue policies at those low premiums, but in time the marketplace proved otherwise and all companies began to sell very inexpensive Term Insurance.

Similar changes occurred in all other products, which is a normal reaction to open competition. The bottom line was the load and the profit margins on life insurance products shrunk dramatically. This also resulted in many agents being forced, for defensive reasons, to sell products outside of their primary company. Their clients wouldn't buy the higher-premium plans and if they did, there was a fair chance they'd lapse the policy when they discovered they could get it for a lot less elsewhere. This increased the volume of brokerage production.

I became aware of this evolving change when a very good friend of mine, Harry Guttman, called me in 1974 and asked me to join Al Howes and himself to discuss something he really didn't understand. Up until that point in time any replacement of a life insurance policy was unacceptable. It was called twisting and was both unethical and illegal. That was because it was almost always to the disadvantage of the policyholder, and the agent made a new commission. When Harry, Al, and I met he shared with us something that didn't seem to make sense. He had sold, some years before, an excellent policy for the time, to one of his best clients, using Mutual of New York, his primary company. Some competing broker had gotten to the client and looked at that policy and had done a proposal for a new policy recommending replacing the old and it appeared to be significantly better in both benefits, cost, and cash accumulation. Harry couldn't believe it. He felt there had to be something wrong. Al and I looked at the proposal and frankly came to the same conclusion. There was no reason *not* to replace the old policy, which was until that time considered to be heresy. Of course, since those days, it's become almost standard practice. As a result, all practitioners today must be sure that the policies that we sell are competitive and appropriate, or we can fully expect to be facing a lapse or a replacement down the line.

Change was accelerating. At about the same time lots of things began to occur. Companies began to look at variable products as a standard part of their portfolio. Many got involved in selling mutual funds as well as different investments. Tax shelters, oil and gas, and real estate became very popular and were sold by financial service people of all persuasions. Convergence had begun. All the different financial service firms began to expand their portfolio into product lines, which previously had been exclusively sold by their competitors. Banks, investment houses, real estate firms, and all forms of insurance representatives began to expand their portfolios to include a completely diversified product portfolio. Of course great numbers of practitioners were still yelling "Tradition!" but the handwriting was on the wall and it accelerated in the 80's, and by the 90's almost everybody was selling just about everything.

In the Life Insurance industry, the traditional companies were forced to cut expenses in order to compete. With cost-cutting came a cutback in education and training and agent support, and in many companies, recruiting. Recruiting was perceived by some to not only be expensive, which was part of the reason for the cutback, but retention of the recruits became a major problem. Brokerage had raised its head and agents were frequently subsidized into the business by one company and either brokered much of their business or, once they reached a point of reasonable maturity, would leave that company and go elsewhere. Fortunately not all companies stopped recruiting and several continued to do it the traditional way and actually prospered. But many companies abandoned the career distribution system and went into full-fledged brokerage operations.

> In the Life Insurance industry, the traditional companies were forced to cut expenses in order to compete.

Agents who enjoyed working in an environment with other agents but who were now independent and no longer associated with a primary company, formed producer groups. They would then negotiate with some of the brokerage companies for special products and special compensation. Many of the larger producers in the insurance business went that route.

This overview of the 20th century does not include what has happened that's good, and what has happened that's bad. The rest of this book will be dedicated to trying to recapture what was good and point out what perhaps was bad. There is no question that technology and the evolution I've described have contributed to the total financial service industry being in the best position it has ever enjoyed. This is certainly so in the case of the consumer and the dedicated, professional advisor. On the other hand, many of the valuable traditional skills and techniques in the sociological environment in which we now work have been lost because of the time and attention dedicated to accommodating these dramatic changes.

The 21st century financial advisor is clearly in the best position any financial advisor has ever enjoyed in the history of our financial service industry; but in my opinion, as good as it is, it could be even better if we recaptured some of the wonders of the Golden Years.

Chapter 2

THE WAY IT IS

It is certainly different. But before I specifically address changes in the financial service business, changes that have occurred in our great nations are of even greater concern.

The very foundation of everything I believe about the financial service industry is based on a broad premise that, in fact, the financial service business is the last bastion of the free enterprise system. I believed it when I was a salesman selling only life insurance in the insurance industry, and I believed it even more when I learned to diversify my product line and to evolve into a financial advisor.

The basis of this belief is that our great country is based on the free enterprise system, and that system presumes that every individual will have the opportunity to build their own well-being and long-term financial security because of their capacity to perform and produce. I predicted 50 years ago that if that system didn't provide adequate security and protection for the American public the only alternative was Government. I further suggested that if that responsibility ever fell to Government and Government then provided the necessary well-being and security, not only would the free enterprise system fail, but we would end up with a nation of dependents totally obligated to the Government, which would eventually itself fall into insolvency and self destruction. Hence, the observation that the financial service arena is, in fact, the last bastion of the free enterprise system because if it fails, Government would have to intercede and, in time, Government itself would also fail.

In the context of this chapter, "The Way It Is," I fear that we are going down a road leading to the destruction of our economic system and therefore, our nation. In the Golden Years of sharing and giving that was not a likely scenario, but in today's environment of 'What's in it for me?' and expectations of entitlement, the threat is very real. Politicians seem to be more concerned with getting the vote and reelected than with the well-being of our nation. Entitlements have become a way of life. The systems already in place, including Social Security and Medicare, are grossly underfunded, with more and more people receiving and fewer and fewer paying into the system.

Corporate and Government pension plans are frightfully underfunded, and some day we'll have to pay the piper. Municipalities and the State and Federal governments provide pension benefits that are totally unrealistic and, again, totally underfunded. We can ignore the problem until it becomes a crisis, but by then it's likely to be too late.

I can remember during the Depression years hearing about countries in Europe where it would take bundles of paper money to get a loaf of bread and though it may have been an exaggeration, a wheelbarrow full of money, to buy anything of substance. Some day we are going to have to either grossly devaluate our money, or significantly change the present entitlement programs, so that the payouts are within the capacity of governments and corporations. Both have been unpopular choices, and most politicians would rather procrastinate than do what's right for fear of losing votes. Something will have to be done eventually, and I hope it will be done sooner rather than later to preserve this greatest nation on Earth before it's too late.

However, it became the greatest nation based on the free enterprise system. As an example insurance companies were committed to providing quality and security for their policyholders. Stock options for employees and executives and high levels of compensation were not part of the game. Building a long-time field organization of successful practitioners was an investment that companies were prepared to make. It is self-evident that the industry, in many cases, has forgotten its mission and is solely concerned with survivorship, then profitability, and finally self-serving benefits, rather than providing security for the American public.

> However, it became the greatest nation based on the free enterprise system.

The light at the end of this very dark tunnel is still the financial service industry. Only if our industry can rededicate itself to providing security for the American public when faced with the three inevitable risks – dying too soon, living too long, and the hazards along the way – on an individual self-providing basis, can our nation succeed economically in the long run. Despite the frightful under-funding of current benefits in both the corporate and Government level, there are many individuals demanding additional entitlements that they have not earned and by paying their fair share. There is no question that it would be in the best interests of all concerned if there was no poverty, everyone had health insurance, employment was available for all, and the Government's concern was limited to providing for those who are incapable of providing for themselves.

Things like tenure, guaranteed benefits regardless of productivity and performance, and free handouts, often to people who have not paid into the system, cannot and should not exist in light of the current circumstances. In today's world, the way it now is, mediocrity and performance, and entitlements for all, along with exorbitant underfunded benefit commitments are leading our great nation down the road of eventual bankruptcy.

The good news is that qualified financial advisors should recognize the vulnerability of the present system and should dedicate themselves to filling those vacuums for every individual they meet. Only through the effective use of the free enterprise system, which made our nation great, can we survive in the future.

We will revisit each of the different financial persuasions in this chapter and acknowledge the many changes that have occurred. It is fair to say some of the changes have made things the best they have ever been and are almost all for the good. There are other changes, which perhaps from the perspective of our mission are not so good. It is not the purpose of this chapter to be a critic, or to editorialize; it is simply to describe the financial service business as it now is and the changes that have impacted on the current financial advisor business.

The real estate business has been very interesting. During the period of change in the last century, real estate appeared in the portfolios of many of the financial persuasions who were going toward diversification from specialization. Real estate investment trusts were very popular for a while. Tax sheltered limited partnership investments in real estate were also favorably perceived during the 70's and 80's.

Commercial real estate business went up and down, and during the boom days, major investors made lots of money, but in the downturns, some major investors were literally forced into bankruptcy.

In today's world, real estate is back to being bought and then used or sold, hopefully at a profit. Real estate salesmen have proliferated. As an example: I live in Palm Springs, which is part of the Coachella Valley. We have a full-time population of over 300,000 people that doubles in the winter months when the "snow-birds" come down for part-time living and to get away from the frigid cold weather in the North. There are over 3,000 real estate salespeople in our valley, many of whom sell very little, if any, real estate in any given year. They look for friends and relatives to give them business, but they cannot be described as true professionals. I personally have many friends who are licensed to sell real estate, which is pretty typical of the situation for most of the full-time residents. When the time came to either buy or sell my home, I sought the most qualified and competent real estate salesperson among my many acquaintances that were licensed in real estate.

The reaction of those I did not choose was not always warm and friendly. Some just acted cool when they found I had chosen a different realtor. One in particular never spoke to me again. That individual was probably the least competent of all the people I knew in the business, and I was aware that he had actually badly mishandled some real estate situations for some mutual friends. Nonetheless, from that point forward, he would never speak to me, which apparently was not an uncommon thing for the unprofessional real estate representative. Frankly, this environment reminded me of the way it was in the insurance business when I joined that industry 60 years ago. There were more licensed life insurance agents than the market could handle, and many of them depended on friends and relatives to squeeze out a minimal income in a very unprofessional way.

New construction of real estate properties has continued both in the residential and the commercial areas at an extremely rapid pace. Shopping malls and commercial buildings have boomed from coast to coast, and fortunes have been made by people who had the vision to exploit the opportunity. In the residential area, the Levittown type development slowly evolved from bare-bone, minimum housing and now provides respectable low-income housing all the way up to the very luxurious country club condominiums and private homes. Many new developments are now fenced with security gates and may have clubhouses, swimming pools, and tennis courts. As a matter of fact, in my Coachella Valley, there are well over 100 golf courses currently in action, and the great majority are private courses for members or homeowners in that specific gated community.

Inflation has heavily impacted the residential market, and houses today cost hundreds of thousands into the millions, instead of the less than $10,000 of the post-war development; but with modern conveniences and beautiful architectural layouts, most current residential properties are rather extraordinary.

I believe in time, as it has in the insurance industry, the number of real estate agents will be significantly reduced, partially by the marketplace and partially by regulation and perhaps continuing education. On the positive side, the consumer is able to buy the best housing ever available in the most comfortable environment.

Banking has changed even more. The impressive, monumental-type buildings still exist for a few home-office banks, but the great majority of bank branches could be anywhere and at any place. Some of them are in stand-alone buildings, some are in commercial properties down at the street level, and some are even in supermarkets. The many tellers behind cages have been replaced in large part by automatic teller machines or "ATM's," where the bank client can make deposits and withdrawals without ever talking to a live human being. Bank tellers are not behind caged enclosures, but on the other side of the counter or sitting at a desk; regrettably, they are no more knowledgeable or qualified to give advice on financial matters than they were 60 years ago. Most bank branches have some personnel called managers who are available for more complex questions, and it's necessary to speak to them directly to get information involving anything out of the ordinary. The teller also must get permission from their manager to do some basic actions if the amounts involved exceed their authorization. Almost all banks now have a diversity of products addressing the financial needs of their clients. Annuities are commonplace, many have insurance, and all offer advice on retirement and loans. They have so-called specialists available for those types of transactions. The trust company part of banking has significantly expanded and personal banking and working with the Trust Department is now available for all bank customers, particularly the more affluent clients. The Federal Government with its FDIC insurance plan guarantees deposits up to $100,000 per individual, and by using Trusts, or multiple owners, that number can be significantly increased. That guarantee attracts depositors who are then prepared to get a more conservative rate of return, but with Government-backed safety.

Banking has changed even more.

Traditional banking interest rates have on occasion, over the last 50 years, spiked to higher levels, but most of the time they have been just a couple of points above the rate of inflation. During this same period, other investment vehicles generate higher rates of return than bank savings interest rates, but with greater downside risks. All that notwithstanding, bank certificates of deposit, money-market deposits, and regular savings accounts are still very popular for clients with a low risk tolerance level.

The impact of diversification, or what is now known as 'convergence,' has significantly increased the bank's portfolios. Despite bank products still being part of the foundation of most peoples' financial plan, they have had a minimal impact on the effectiveness of investment brokers or insurance people. Without an improvement in their personal skill level in interpersonal relationships with their customers, and concurrently utilizing their diversified modern portfolio along with their relatively modest, conservative investment returns, that is not likely to change in the foreseeable future. Nonetheless, the potential for banks to become more aggressive, more sophisticated, and more competent at giving financial advice could make them a major player in the financial advising business.

Investment brokers have aggressively diversified and now have in their portfolios all of the financial instruments. However, most of the individual brokers have remained specialists. They are primarily still selling, stocks, bonds, mutual funds, and variable annuities.

During the transitional period of change, and during part of the last century, some individuals and organizations aggressively marketed what were known as "junk bonds." These were bonds paying high rates of interest to offset the apparent security risk of the issuing companies. Many junk bond specialists made lots of money, but some went a bit too far misrepresenting their products and ended up in jail.

Mutual funds became an acceptable and popular product because it gave the small investor a way of having lots of eggs in the basket and benefiting from the general upward trend in the market. The commissions and the marketing had become reasonable and proper, although there had been some marketing techniques that were frowned on in the latter half of the 20th century that is now long-forgotten. Today most financial institutions and all financial advisors, regardless of their former specialization, include mutual funds in their portfolio.

One of the impacts of 'convergence' and 'diversification' on the overall industry is each of the different specialty persuasions brought with them some of the methodology that was typical of their business. As an example: proselytizing in the life insurance industry was a dirty word. Companies invested a lot of money to bring in potential recruits and then took the time and trouble to educate and train them. They frequently subsidized their income in anticipation of developing a sales organization, which would be loyal to the recruiting company. Until the last part of the 20th century, proselytizing agents from an insurance company that made this substantial investment in the development of that salesperson by another company was seriously frowned upon. I can remember when George Joseph, who had been a Vice President for New England Mutual and then became President of the company organization now known as LIMRA, the Life Insurance Marketing Research Association, spoke at an industry meeting and aggressively denigrated proselytizing companies. He called them parasites and got a standing ovation. In today's world, many companies have built, and are continuing to build, their sales organization by seducing either career agents from companies that are still doing the recruiting or offering incentives to independent agents to get them to transfer their production to their company. I suspect this might have happened in the current environment without the impact of the investment industry, but this practice was pretty common and totally acceptable in the investment industry and I suspect had an impact on accelerating the progress of what we used to call proselyting to all aspects of the financial service business. We will discuss this again when we talk about the life insurance business later in this chapter.

Marketing in the investment part of the business is still heavily influenced by dialing and smiling. The individual broker/salesperson does a good part of their marketing by calling potential prospects and offering them what sound like fantastic investment opportunities. They're likely to mention tax advantages, high rates of return, tremendous potential for appreciation, or steady growth. I suspect, besides myself, almost every other person in the United States gets phone calls from investment brokers who always have deals too good to refuse. Even for the qualified professional investment advisor who has an established clientele, the telephone is the primary marketing tool. If done with persistence and aggressiveness over a long enough period of time, it works, and many people in the investment field have become very successful without actually having met a significant part of their clientele.

The Property and Casualty insurance business, which has now embraced all financial products, and many companies who are now called multi-line, have expanded greatly. Several of the major companies, with captive sales representatives, have really prospered over the past 50 years. State Farm is a classic example of great success. They have enrolled large numbers of highly qualified practitioners who run their own business as entrepreneurs and who have, on average, very substantial incomes. They have changed the diversity of their sales organization and now have significant numbers of women representatives and people representing every race, color, and creed. In some ways they have become a model for the other companies doing much the same thing. Farmers Insurance, Farm Bureau Companies, Allstate, Nationwide, and others have similar marketing systems and have also been quite successful.

The biggest challenge they've all had was that their long-time representatives were only comfortable selling their Property and Casualty coverage. That coverage now has been consolidated to where homeowner policies are all-inclusive, as are automobile policies and it's a somewhat simpler business. As the President of State Farm once told me, the big difference between marketing Property and Casualty insurance and Life insurance is for Life Insurance you have to create a sale where none previously existed. In Property and Casualty insurance, everyone already has homeowners insurance or automobile insurance. All a company can do in their marketing is try to attract that insurance away from their competitors based on service, advertising, and cost. For that reason, there is relatively little sharing of ideas and methodology between the Property and Casualty companies, since each considers their techniques their own domain. In the end, they're all essentially chasing the same policies from the same consumers and rarely creating a new sale.

Considerable stress was put on the Property and Casualty companies during the last part of the 20th century and the first part of the 21st. There have been some catastrophic natural events, earthquakes, landslides, floods, storms, and mammoth fires, which have resulted in tremendous property and casualty claims. As a result, many of the Property and Casualty companies have become far more cautious in what coverage they will write and who they will write it on. In many instances, companies have completely shut down large geographical territories from the issuing of new automobile, homeowners, or earthquake insurance where the perceived risk level seemed too high. In order for the companies to continue to survive in those areas, it became necessary for them to more aggressively market products that were not affected by those property and casualty losses. Not necessarily solely because of this, but as part of an expanded marketing plan, most captive agent multi-line companies have enlarged their portfolios to include investments and life insurance products. This allowed their representatives to continue to sell and make money in areas where there was a freeze on certain parts of their portfolio. It also represented a new substantial potential for economic growth. As a result, most captive agents representing multi-line companies have become far more sophisticated and expert at marketing products other than property and casualty insurance and that trend is likely to continue into the future.

Since the late 60's, I have actually been a practitioner incorporating all of the above-mentioned financial products, but my early emphasis was as a life insurance specialist. I lived through the transition of the life insurance industries evolution and its marketing has changed tremendously. My organization and I were considered pioneers in this movement, though there have been some traumatic times.

For example, it was always felt that life insurance companies were absolutely safe from a financial point of view. They had accumulated great wealth, but many things happened over the past 30 or 40 years that affected that situation. In the latter part of the 20th century inflation and interest rates skyrocketed at times. Traditional life insurance products had guaranteed interest rates and guaranteed loan rates built into the structure. People were hard-pressed for money and utilized a technique I had never heard of until that time – "disintermediation." They went to their life insurance company and borrowed money at a guaranteed lower rate of interest, and then invested it elsewhere at a higher rate of interest and made money on their borrowed money. Many life insurance companies were facing the stress of tremendous amounts of cash going out and relatively little coming in, and extremely high interest rates if they needed to borrow cash.

Concurrently, the cost of doing business was increasing steadily because of inflation. The premiums on their existing life insurance had been calculated anticipating a lower cost for doing business and provided loan provisions to the policy holder at low guaranteed interest rates. This was a double financial hit at life insurance companies during a high interest inflationary time. Also, brokerage business had become a major marketing threat. Companies were developing new products at very low premiums. In order to compete, the traditional companies had to figure out actuarially how to cut costs, enjoy improved mortality, and invest assets at higher rates of interest in order to produce products that were competitive in the marketplace. With premiums down, and borrowing up, a cash crunch was inevitable. This was a combination that was nearly catastrophic for some companies. Fortunately before any companies failed, though several were severely shaken, and before any serious harm was done, interest rates came down and disintermediation was no longer an attractive vehicle for exploiting existing life insurance.

Concurrently, the cost of doing business was increasing steadily because of inflation.

By then, variable products were on the horizon and the investment companies developed a new product known as Universal Life. Both the variable products and Universal Life gave the companies an opportunity to produce very attractive products, with lower premiums and more of the risk transferred from the company to the policy holder.

Field agents who were unfamiliar with anything except guaranteed products quickly discovered this made the life insurance product a much easier sale. Prospects enjoyed the opportunity to pay lower premiums and still have the advantage of benefiting from the appreciation of investments in the marketplace.

Again, in order to create attractive variable and universal products, some companies became far more aggressive in their own investing practices. Until that time, all companies put almost all of their money in secured conservative rate-of-return-type investments. After these changes, some companies began to explore more aggressive investments in real estate, junk bonds, and other higher rate of return, but also higher risk, investments.

When things were good that worked very well. Companies were able to market products based on new higher anticipated rates of return that looked absolutely phenomenal. But what goes up also comes down. When junk bonds and real estate crashed, the aggressive investment practice companies were in serious financial stress. Also, life insurance companies, with a lot of retirement and wealth accumulation type clients, found themselves at a squeeze for liquidity. Their clients had expectations of having money available any time they wanted it, but money that was tied up in junk bonds or real estate was, at least for the moment, not liquid. A few companies actually went under, others had to structurally re-organize, but the industry rallied to protect the failing companies' policy holders.

Many companies decided to switch from a mutual-type structure where the company was owned by the policy-holders, to a stockholder-owned company where they could get an infusion of capital through the sale of stock, and individual corporate executives could get higher compensation, bonuses, and stock deals. This also made it possible for small companies to be gobbled up by big companies because they were no longer policy-holder owned. Mergers were rampant, so some companies failed and some got merged out of existence. "Economy of scale" was the key to success in the now more competitive business.

To make a bad situation even worse, many salespeople who were unfamiliar with the diversified products now added to their portfolio, misused and abused marketing methods by creating unreasonable projections on the new variable and universal life type policies. In fairness, though it was the practitioners that misrepresented, a good part of the blame falls on the companies themselves for doing an inadequate job of training and educating their people in the new products and then strictly enforcing their recommended methodologies. No matter who was to blame, lawsuits became the name of the game. Some were monster class-action suits, some were just individuals claiming they had purchased products under false pretenses and had been promised benefits they would never receive. Much of that litigation ended in significant judgments against the financial institutions.

Soon thereafter all financial institutions established compliance departments, which were non-existent for most of the last century. The fear of even more litigation, which had already added up to billions of dollars against the different financial institutions, made all companies ultra-conservative. The compliance departments in some ways controlled everything, including marketing. I do not challenge the purpose. It was, and is, well intentioned. However, it is now so rigidly enforced by people that have no idea of the true mission of the financial institutions that marketing financial products, most significantly life insurance and investment type products, has become far more difficult and perhaps the pendulum has swung too far. Clearly, however, this heavy litigation has also affected the well-being of some of the financial institutions, and controls to prevent abuses in the future were necessary.

As companies became stockholder owned, sometimes profit for the stockholder became more important than the mission of providing protection for the consumer. Happily, some of the most highly respected companies have chosen to continue to be primarily dedicated to their customers and have remained mutual companies. They are continuing to recruit and train qualified representatives, despite all the trauma of the past three decades. Some companies that had abandoned the career agent distribution system and tried proselyting and brokerage as an alternative have returned to the career system; but the great majority of companies that formerly recruited and built their own sales organizations of quality, well-trained representatives no longer pursue that route.

Another major change in the life insurance industry was many agents who felt abused by their companies, as the support, training, and motivation diminished, usually because of cost controls, predictably reacted to the basic principle that loyalty begets loyalty. When companies denigrated agents, the agents responded in kind by diminishing their loyalty and commitment to their companies. As a result, many agents from certain companies quit their companies and became independents. Subsequently, some figured out they missed the camaraderie and the support they formerly enjoyed so they created what we now know as 'producer groups.' There are high-level producers or independent entrepreneurs who form alliances, often with the structure of a company, making special arrangements with certain manufacturers of brokerage products to get a better portfolio at better commissions and still conduct their business as entrepreneurs.

On a totally different subject, in the old days that kind of producer probably made more money than the Chief Executive Officer of the company. Under the stock-ownership rules the game changed. Most executives in the companies get stock options and stock bonuses. They've also gotten significant pay increases. As a result, many companies are led by people who had no previous life insurance experience. They are investment people, attorneys, or actuaries, and they are earning, in some instances, multimillions of dollars a year in compensation. If you analyze the compensation of Chief Executive Officers of life insurance companies, you can almost tell from the level of compensation whether the company is a stock company or a mutual company. The traditional mutual companies still pay their executives significantly less than the stock companies.

Another interesting impact of that change is that, as I suggested above, companies that have chosen to become money-making machines for stockholders frequently cut back on all expenses that do not directly lead to short term profit. That frequently includes training and education, development of new sales personnel, management personnel, and advertising and public relations. The companies that are still recruiting and developing people and are investing in their future are to be commended. Lest this not be misunderstood, there are some great stock companies and there are some marginal mutual companies. I am not advocating either approach, I am simply suggesting that there have been significant changes and among the changes are trends that concern me about the well-being of the industry in the future.

At the marketing level, again much has changed. All sales presentations must be approved by Compliance. Computers have replaced calculators and typewriters. All correspondence and all material must be approved by Compliance and it's all the representatives can use. All incoming and outgoing mail or proposals and illustrations, everything happening, has to pass Compliance.

Executives in the Home Office and Compliance departments, along with a push for cost controls, have shifted marketing leadership away from the most important person in the distribution of financial products for life insurance companies. The key person for recruiting and developing agents was always the agency manager.

Of course, in the companies that have maintained the career agency system as their primary distributions system, the manager is still the key person, but even in those companies the managers position and job description is substantially different. In other than career companies, it is almost purely administrative.

Compliance, cost controls, administration, and technological applications all can consume most of a managers time. Selling skills, the miracle of the product, motivation, inspiration, accountability of the producer, the so-called "religion" of the business, goal-setting, planning, levels of activity, prospecting, etc., in many companies and agencies, are lost skills. They are lost for two reasons. The manager doesn't have them, or doesn't have time for them with the new job descriptions, and the financial advisor producer isn't getting them because the proper source of this coaching has always been the manager.

Company training programs and educational programs have been eliminated in many, but thankfully, not all companies, and the agency manager often is not capable or inclined to fill that vacuum.

GAMA and it's foundation, at it's annual LAMP meetings and in it's research projects, has available the information and techniques to fill that vacuum, but the continuing erosion of the role of the agency manager must be reversed for the industry to survive and prosper with a profitable and productive distribution system.

Prospecting methods have also been impacted. The 'Do Not Call' concept has been introduced, and if an individual takes their telephone off of the allowed-to-call list you can no longer do phone solicitation. Direct mail has been heavily utilized with an ever-decreasing effectiveness. E-mail on the computer has become a major communication vehicle and everyone carries a laptop, or at the very least, has a desktop computer in their office and perhaps their home.

Prospecting methods have also been impacted.

When Harry Guttman came to me and asked if it seemed correct that an old life insurance policy could be replaced by a new life insurance policy and still be to the advantage of the policyholder, the inquiry was revolutionary. Up until then 'twisting,' which is what that practice was called, was illegal and unethical. However, with the new policies that were introduced and the reduction in premiums, a by-product of everything we've been talking about in this chapter, it turned out that there are many situations where a new policy is better for the policyholder than an old one. Twisting disappeared from our vocabulary and for a period of time replacements became quite commonplace. Eventually most policies that should have been replaced were replaced and the level of activity fell dramatically. On the other hand, certain requirements were established to make sure that the replacement wasn't simply to make a new commission for the salesperson, but rather in the best interests of the policyholder.

Much of this chapter sounds negative but actually, because of the changes, things have never been better. Today there are more people with more money and more financial problems than ever before in history. At the same time, because of attrition in the numbers of people in the industry and things like continuing education requirements and the basic survival of the fittest concepts, there are fewer financial advisors, and they are better qualified than they have ever been. All of this is happening because of the free enterprise system. Because of competition the products now available are the best products at the lowest prices ever available. The product-pusher of yesteryear was relatively uneducated and untrained and like myself, had to learn selling someplace else or fail, but today has evolved into a financial advisor with more skill, more knowledge, and with a better diversified portfolio than ever before. The consumer is clearly better served and is more aware of the need for good financial advice. Companies are settling down and figuring out how they plan to market in the future and what they must do to develop a distribution system that can be effective.

Convergence has resulted in banks, investment people, property and casualty and multi-line agents, and life insurance agents all becoming financial advisors. They each have a very complete portfolio to address the three main risks that all people face – living too long, dying too soon, and the hazards that occur along the way. The economy as a trend has consistently gone up, and that includes real estate, the stock market, or standard of living. With modern communication the consumer has become far more sophisticated and is more aware of the problems they're going to face economically in the future. The baby-boomer generations are no longer babies and, as I write this, the eldest of them are beginning to enter the era of retirement, and they will be facing more problems than most have been prepared to address and desperately need good advice and counsel.

In these global times, the MDRT and GAMA have both become international and have significant numbers of members all over the world participating in their programs and communicating with each other. Compliance, legislation, and regulation have tightened the parameters under which the financial advisor-practitioner operates, resulting in a much higher quality professional approach to client interpersonal relationships. Some of the great life insurance companies are recruiting new agents, and they are doing it at a higher level of sophistication than ever before, and the multi-line companies and fraternal companies are aggressively recruiting and expanding their sales organizations with a far more demographically diversified group of representatives.

More and more representatives are earning academic designations through proper educational institutions to improve their knowledge along with their skill. The LUTCF, the Life Underwriter Training Counsel Fellow; the CLU, Chartered Life Underwriter designation of the American College, along with the ChFC, Chartered Financial Consultant; the CFP designation; and the RFC, Registered Financial Consultant designation have all become a minimal expectation of any qualified financial advisor.

I am reminded of a story I heard some time ago that I'm told was true. The Texaco Oil Company, which was advertising on the Milton Berle television show, decided to aggressively promote their product and increase sales. They called in consultants and the advertising people suggested that people on the road liked to find clean restrooms at the gas stations and they should feature that they had the cleanest gas stations in America. This was on television and in the newspapers. Surprisingly, sales didn't go up, they went down. Texaco again called in the consultants and said, "What's happening? We've spent a fortune on advertising and it hasn't helped sales. The sales went down."

So the consulting firm went out and did some field investigation. They came back to Texaco with the following story. They said it wasn't the problem with the concept of the advertising campaign. Clean restrooms would sell gasoline. The problem was that when people went into the Texaco restrooms, they found they were filthy and presumed that if the company was lying about the cleanliness of their restrooms, they were also lying about the quality of their gasoline. You see, you don't advertise a concept to the public without being prepared to deliver the concept. If Texaco had first cleaned the restrooms and then done the advertising, it would have been an effective campaign.

Our industry has been through a slow evolution, an accelerated evolution, and then a revolution, and we were bruised and battered along the way. Lots of bad things happened, but we've cleaned up our act. Today our restrooms, so to speak, are clean. We have the best field force addressing problems that have to be addressed, and the future has never looked brighter.

In the next chapter however, I will spend some time sharing some of the things we've lost in this painful evolution/revolution that would be of value for the 21st century practitioner. I will also, in subsequent chapters, discuss in great detail different skills and techniques that are as, or perhaps even more, appropriate today as they were in the Golden Years but have been neglected along the way. In the end the reader will have a roadmap to follow to have more fun, make more money, and do a better job for the consumer in the 21st century, by utilizing the timeless techniques developed in the 20th century.

Chapter 3

THE WAY IT COULD AND SHOULD BE

There is no question that many things in the 21st century are far better than they were at any time in the 20th. The technological advancements are spectacular and as a byproduct of change, the products available to the consumer are the best they've ever been. Also, as a result of change, many former practitioners who are not qualified to professionally advise the consumer have either been terminated or voluntarily resigned from the financial service business.

The product-pushing salesperson of yesterday is being replaced by the knowledgeable professional totally diversified financial advisor, which is certainly an important step in the right direction. In that context, since financial advisors come from many different financial institutions, my observations, in this chapter and all of the subsequent chapters, are appropriate for financial advisors, whether they represent banks, investment houses, multiple-line companies, independent property and casualty brokers, and certainly people representing life and health insurance companies. These remarks are even appropriate for the new generation of mortgage brokers who are only marginally in the total financial advising business but who nonetheless are aggressively soliciting new mortgages, refinancing existing mortgages, and selling reverse mortgages, which in each instance help with the consumer's cash flow. Certainly, fee-based financial advisors, and even accountants and attorneys would benefit from some of the ideas included in the subsequent chapters in this book.

> The product-pushing salesperson of yesterday is being replaced by the knowledgeable professional totally diversified financial advisor.

However, before we get to the specific skills and techniques that will be addressed in subsequent chapters, I would like to share some thoughts about the total environment in which financial advisors currently practice. These observations will be directed primarily on things that have existed in the past, particularly in the Golden Years, and have been lost or forgotten because of the impact of change. I believe I am a realist and recognize much of what I will discuss in this chapter may never happen, but as I say in the chapter title, I believe it could and should.

I will never forget a speech I heard at the Million Dollar Round Table (MDRT), where the presenter suggested anything that has ever been done is not impossible. It took 20 to 30 years to dramatically change the financial advising business, so I don't think it is unrealistic to believe that in the next decade or two much of what I'm going to refer to in this chapter could conceivably be re-incorporated into our fantastic business. I believe the basic fact that convergence is here to stay and every financial institution should significantly diversify their product lines to incorporate all financial products. The problem, however, is that you don't become a financial advisor by simply changing your name and diversifying your portfolio. Individuals who were originally specialty product salespeople and who represent companies that were once known and recognized as specialty product producers often find it difficult to change and adapt to the new world. They say you can't change the spots on a leopard, but the human being is adaptable and flexible and can be anything he or she wants to be.

I will give some details on how to adapt to this transition in the chapter on the evolution of the financial service business. For the moment, let me simply suggest that the future world of financial advisors should be dedicated to the mission of objectively providing the consumer with protection against all three risks – dying too soon, living too long, and the hazards that occur along the way. This means becoming sensitive to the consumer's wants and aspirations and being completely open minded in recommending the best product to solve each of those risks, even if it's outside the advisors initial comfort zone.

The next question of course is where are these financial advisors of the future going to come from? Many companies have abandoned new advisor recruiting and are building sales forces by attracting, or perhaps I should say seducing, representatives from other companies to resign and join their organization. This is not an editorial to stop the individual practitioner from making a career decision in his or her best interest. It is, however, expressing a concern about a trend that is leading to fewer and fewer people in the business and very few young people coming in. When I spoke at financial organizational meetings in the past, I can remember when the average age was in the 30s, perhaps the 40s, with a significant number of new people in their 20s and 30s. Today when I speak, the majority of the attendees are in their 50s, and there are relatively few people in attendance who are in their first three years as financial advisors.

There are multiple potential solutions to that problem. First, I truly believe new advisor recruiting, with a structure not unlike the life insurance industry's agency system, is still a viable method of marketing and distribution. Companies that have continued to perform using that structure have prospered. Another possibility is that independent advisors could build their own organizations and recruit and develop using their own expertise to transfer the skills from generation to generation.

I was fortunate to be the Chairman of the MDRT Mentoring Committee, which conceived, created, and implemented, eventually in partnership with the General Agents and Managers Association, the mentoring program currently in place. Where it has been effectively used, it has been tremendously successful. Several companies have embraced it but many others have not. The mentoring of new people coming into this business by successful entrepreneurs who are already successfully performing is the best resource for transferring skills from one generation to the next. Management and company people often don't have the necessary people skills of the field practitioner. It is mutually beneficial for the company, the mentor, the aspirant, and the consumer to improve and/or develop the skills and knowledge of all practitioners. It is also economically beneficial since the records show that the mentor, along with the aspirant, enjoy improved productivity and income while having more fun.

The multi-line companies, who develop entrepreneurial, though captive representatives for their companies, are aggressively recruiting and building advisors for the future.

However, since most companies have cut back or eliminated training and education, that vacuum has to be filled. Perhaps the National Association of Insurance and Financial Advisors (NAIFA) or the General Agents and Managers Association (GAMA) could fill that vacuum by creating a career path training and educational program available for all financial advisors. They could incorporate existing programs, such as The American College, The Life Underwriters Training Council, and the CFP programs, but they could be the distribution system, coordination, and accountability leaders.

That brings up the subject of continuing education. I was Chairman of the NALU, now NAIFA. Educational Program when we mandated education as a pre-requisite for being a member of the organization. Clearly, I embrace continuing education. However in my opinion, the pendulum, as it has in many areas, has swung too far. Of course we need continuing education, but success for the practitioner is equally dependent on skill and motivation. Neither of those subjects generates continuing education credits. As a result, many meetings that are available to practitioners use continuing education hours as an inducement for attendance and, slowly, over the years have all but eliminated programs addressing inter-personal skills and providing motivation and inspiration for the practitioner. It frustrates me when I am asked to speak at a company or industry meeting, and the sponsoring company or organization wants the material to qualify for continuing education and will not allow motivation or skill development subjects. The 21st century practitioner needs inspiration and motivation just as much as the 20th century salesperson, but frankly in most cases, they're not getting it.

As a by-product of that evolvement, I am also aware of the vacuum created by the heroes of yesterday dying and retiring and very few visible heroes coming forth in the modern day generation. You might ask, "What do I mean by hero?" Let me share my perception of industry heroes, the wonderful super stars of another time who should never be forgotten.

The following list of heroes includes personal friends, many of whom are gone, some happily are still with us, but all gave of themselves freely to make this a better place.

The likes of Lyle Blessman, Fred Donaldson, Mehdi Fakharzadeh, Marvin Feldman, Ben Feldman, Charlie Flowers, Dave Fluegelman, Tony Gordon, Al Granum, Bart Hodges, Al Howes, Kirke Lewis, Stan Liss, Van Mueller, Julian Myrick, Frank Nathan, Jack Peckinpaugh, Lester Rosen, John Savage, Ben Silver, Gary Sitzmann, C. Carney Smith, Frank Sullivan, Grant Taggart, John Todd, John Utz, Tom Wolff, Dave Woods, Woody Woodson, Buddy Zais, Roger Zener, and Charlie Zimmerman. They left a legacy that far exceeds in value their tremendous economic impact on our industry. There are of course many more 20th century heroes, but I only listed those special people I could call friend.

These wonderful heroes still walk the halls of every industry meeting because their passion, ideas, and techniques were passed on to tens of thousands of practitioners who sat at their feet. These tremendous protégés are the successful practitioners of today.

But what about tomorrow? With companies recruiting far fewer people, with training programs, in many cases, as dead as the Dodo, and with managers overwhelmed with compliance and cost controls and sadly deficient in sales skills, who is filling the vacuum created by the loss of yesterday's heroes? Where are the volunteer practitioners who are extraordinarily successful and have the skill to communicate and motivate others, who are spending a significant amount of time and energy sharing their passion and expertise?

But what about tomorrow?

Happily there are a few, but very few, at a time when we need more of them than ever in our industry's history.

Those of us who served in World War II have been lauded as a special generation. In retrospect, that may well be true. We enthusiastically entered the service of our country and gave whatever we were capable of giving for the cause. We were unselfish and never questioned our country's call.

Until now, I never made the analogy, but that was the same in our financial service industry. We came, we struggled, and some survived. Those of us who did were happy about sharing and giving back to this fantastic industry. We got as much pleasure from giving as we derived from taking. We didn't ask to be paid, but enthusiastically volunteered. As a result, we had more fun and made more money than one could have attained in any other profession.

Also as a result of this volunteerism, every name I mentioned at the start of this subject was a close personal friend. How do you beat that for fringe compensation?

Being part of that special world, I can share how this came to be. First, as I already suggested, my generation wanted to give back unselfishly. Also, we knew we were in a marathon, not a sprint, and we were comfortable investing in the long run, not just for the moment. We were all active in our local Life Underwriter groups, and we aspired to get to the Million Dollar Round Table. We joined Study Groups of our peers and learned to both share with our fellow members and receive back in kind. We loved our business and were all missionaries bringing in new talent and helping the new kids on the block. There was no cutthroat competition, and we lived with professional dignity. Our managers encouraged us (and perhaps even required us) to join the local Life Underwriter group, and they and our peers always attended every meeting. Many among us happily volunteered for positions in that organization.

So what has changed? Nearly everything. Many people today want everything today, or perhaps yesterday. We compete, we don't freely share. Managers are afraid of proselytizing and don't encourage their representatives to mingle with the perceived competition. They are too busy to go to the meetings, and it is a low-level priority with immediate survival number one. MDRT has lost a little of it's glamour, as the big hitters are no longer visible or showcased.

Thankfully, it is not all that way. There are some great organizations with great leaders who are still building the old fashioned way. They are truly great in every way. Not only do they do all the right things, they are also unbelievably successful. Maybe that's because they are doing all the right things, and their people are participating in the whole gamut of industry activities.

The MDRT has a great program, providing top producers as speakers at local NAIFA meetings. As yet, not enough of this is being done, but it is an encouraging start.

These are all indications that many leaders in our industry recognize the problem of the lost heroes and are at least starting activities to address the problem. Unfortunately, it is just a tiny beginning, but all great movements began with modest starts.

So it is not impossible to get back some of the religion and passion of yesterday. It's been done, so it isn't impossible. Can you get that involved and still be a great business success? The names in this article have done it, and they have been among the most successful people in our industry.

In all things, we build on the foundation of yesterday. The ghosts of those that came before are the foundation on which we all build. The agents of tomorrow deserve no less from you of the 'today generation'.

Before getting off this subject, let me ask "Heroes for whom?" I know even today the successful practitioners and the superstars have role models to emulate. We are fortunate to have them among us. However, how many of those heroes are even remotely known to the struggling new agent, or multiple-line producer, or the fraternal organizations representatives? How many of them speak at local life underwriter associations five times, or perhaps 20 or 30 times a year? How many of them attend the annual NAIFA meeting and mix with the front line troops?

When I came into the business, I quickly learned the names of the industry heroes and, in short order, had the opportunity to see them in person at local life underwriter meetings, sales congresses, and at company meetings. I read about them in magazines, read their books, listened to their tapes, and heard about them from my successful friends who attended MDRT and other national meetings. They quickly became my role models and the inspiration to become a success in my own practice. When I reached that goal, I instinctively began to give back. I spoke at meetings; one year over 100 times. I wrote books and, until this day, attend both national and local meetings.

The point, of course, is that the types of hero from my generation are significantly less visible in current times. There are a lot of reasons for this, but I believe we still need visible people to follow and therein lay the mission of this message.

Heroes aside, what has the impact of globalization had on the practitioner of today? I can remember shortly after World War II when people from all over the world came to the United States to learn how we marketed and distributed our financial service products. On multiple occasions, I was part of a host group entertaining and sharing ideas with people from Asia, as well as some of the European countries. That was good service, and it has resulted in the financial service industry prospering and expanding all over the world. I'm proud of America's contribution towards that end. I'm also glad that some of our American financial organizations have continued that relationship. However, I am concerned with the internationalization of organizations like the MDRT and the GAMA. While I embrace their intent, my concern is that the practitioners from other countries have different products, certainly different cultural markets, different laws and regulations, and different levels of success. The result has been a significant change in the programming of both of those organizations and an emphasis on attracting significant numbers of members from outside the United States. As I said, I am comfortable with the intent, but I am concerned that the American practitioner is no longer getting the specific ideas that those organizations previously, exclusively offered. My question is not should they no longer be international, but could they have a separate program for American practitioners that provided the specific education, motivation, and inspiration formerly available. I feel a vacuum is being developed that must be filled; perhaps NAIFA could assume that role. I am committed and dedicated to MDRT and GAMA and some American-based programs might solve the problem, but in any case I enjoy participating in their programs.

Their annual meetings were the highlight of my life, but now when I attend, particularly at MDRT, the majority of attendees are not from the Americas. The programming is often directed at the least common denominator. The main platform presentations are dominated by professional speakers not in our industry, and the heroes of yesterday and today are no longer dominant for all attendees. This may be construed as a criticism of the organizations, but it is not. The current administration and all it's predecessors are giving generously of their time as volunteers for the same purposes to which I am committed. It is not a criticism of anything that has been done. It is a wish to bring back and make available some of the magic of the Golden Years for today's practitioners and to do so within the structure of the greatest management and producer organizations in the world.

Compliance is another area that needs to be addressed. I fully understand why companies and the industry felt it necessary to create compliance departments in almost every institution because of the transgressions of some unprofessional practitioners. Unfortunately it had to be done, and I fully understand that it will always be so. However, the power given to those compliance departments is perhaps another example of the pendulum swinging too far. Expensive litigation must be avoided, and compliance must continue to exist. But when non-practitioners, coming from the legal or compliance world, make rules and regulations that are counterproductive to the mission of the company, they become an inhibitor to production and our providing the security for the consumer to which all advisors are dedicated. Some of their work becomes counter-productive.

The question is, if they must continue to exist and exercise controls, what can be done about it? Often compliance decisions take months to make. The likelihood is their answer is going to be 'no' on most issues. Certainly that's not an effective way to carry on the workings of any business.

I've been raised, as a manager, to believe my challenge is to figure out how to use the word 'yes' and get the job done within the restrictions and limitations of the position. I believe Compliance could work much more effectively in cooperation with the marketing and distribution departments of the company. The charge would be to find ways to help the practitioner attain the objective they seek, and to do so, utilizing the limitation and restrictions necessary by the compliance department. Change the 'no's' to 'yes's', and change the time urgency from 'when we get around to it' to 'we'll be back to you next week'. Like I said at the start of this chapter, I believe it could and should be done. I don't expect it to happen anytime soon, but I strongly encourage aggressive movement in that direction.

Another area that has been totally neglected for new financial advisors, which I as a former manager considered my most important responsibility, was seeing to it that the practitioner had somebody watching them and demanding accountability. As an example, the mentoring program of the MDRT/GAMA council was not effective until a monthly reporting form was required of all participants that had to be signed by the mentor, the aspirant, and the manager if there was one. Without that kind of accountability, nothing ever happened. At the very least, every licensed and registered advisor ought to be held to certain minimum standards, with activity, productivity, education, and training and some method of keeping those records should be a requirement. I consider accountability just as important as continuing education and compliance. Actually, they all inter-relate.

When I speak at meetings with as many as thousands of practitioners, and I ask for a show of hands as to how many people see at least 15 people a week, practically no hands go up. At 10, there's little difference. Even when I get to five, the majority of the audience has not raised their hands. When I follow up that question with how many attendees are getting proper fact-finders as a pre-requisite to any potential advising situation, typically less than 10% of the audience raises their hands. My question is: How can someone be a full-time professional financial advisor, certainly in their early years before they establish an affluent clientele, and see fewer than five people a week, and not get fact-finders as a pre-requisite to an on-going advising situation? Companies and agencies no longer have the personnel to discipline the individual practitioner. So once again, we need an industry-wide system, perhaps monitored by NAIFA or delegated to the organization with which the practitioner is affiliated.

A rather challenging change I'd like to see happen is to rebuild loyalty and camaraderie between the individual practitioner, his or her peer group, and the companies they represent. Clearly that existed in the so-called Golden Years. As I already said, loyalty begets loyalty, and the modern generation often only asks, "What's in it for me?" and "How quickly can I get it?" Something is radically wrong.

I don't blame the practitioner. When some companies, particularly in the life insurance business, failed or merged, eliminated the career distribution system and the people it represented, fell behind in the quality of the products they were marketing, and chose leadership that were not committed to the original mission of the financial advising industry, the individual producer responded in kind.

For example, let me share with you my own personal experience. I was completely committed, loyal, and bonded to the companies I represented. I never voluntarily left a company, but here is the history of my career.

> Let me share with you my own personal experience.

I was with my first company, the Aetna Life and Casualty, in the life division for 27 years. Then with change of management, they decided internally and politically to begin to divest themselves of all of their products other than eventually group health insurance. That meant that their life division, which I was part of, was abandoned, then their property and casualty division, and finally they ended up with part of the group division. I was left out in the cold after 27 years of devoted service and had been misrepresented to, because I was told all along the way that their commitment was to the total financial service division.

My second company was Mutual Benefit. This was an over 100-year-old strong, committed to the agency system, life insurance company, that was diversified and had all the products and services I wanted.

I was with Mutual Benefit for 17 years. I was told they were doing great. I was actually encouraged to expand my operation. Then, they went bankrupt. I now know they had been lying to me. When they went bankrupt, they in effect, wiped me out, and I was forced to start all over again.

Next, I went to Sunlife of Canada. Sunlife was a mutual company committed to the agency system in the United States. Sunlife had lots of money and no fear of bankruptcy. Sunlife was Triple-A rated. But after seven years, Sunlife decided to get out of the career distribution system in the United States and become a brokerage company; plus it de-mutualized and became a stock company.

So the three companies that I spent most of my career with, and to each of whom I gave total loyalty and commitment, each misrepresented or changed their mind at some later point in time and ended up abandoning the systems that I bought in the first place. In some instances, the consumer was hurt. In some cases, they weren't. In every instance, the field person was hurt.

It is very difficult to have been hurt by three different companies over a span of more than 50 years, each of whom made promises and commitments and each of whom disappointed me in the end. How can the advisor be loyal to companies when it has been obvious the company and their officers are primarily committed to what they perceive is the best for their own position rather than being concerned for their field organization and the mission to which the company was ostensibly committed.

Another difficult challenge is reintroducing people skills to an industry where many of the different marketing plans currently in existence are product driven. Price, rate of return, tax advantages, promised services, these all have become part of some financial salespeople's presentations. To be an effective advisor, the necessary skill is not based on product, anymore than a doctor builds his or her reputation on the medicine for which they write prescriptions, but rather on the inter-personal relationships and the caring and sharing leading to the customer's well-being. It is rare in the industry today for advisors to be getting skill training in inter-personal relationships.

The financial service industry now has a proliferation of so-called coaches who charge very substantial fees, and probably earn those fees because they're filling a vacuum that should be addressed by the companies the financial advisor represents. They no longer get the direction they need or the skill training they need from their companies, so they are forced to commit to substantial financial costs, besides the time involved, to work with people who profess to be qualified coaches in those areas. Of course, some of them really are, but some are exploiting a vacuum that should be filled within the industry by the financial advising organizations.

Let me conclude this chapter with what I perceive to be the essential truth of financial advising. Whether it is banks, investment houses, insurance companies or whatever, the entire company ought to be committed to a common cause. That commitment and that cause should be providing the public with the best possible financial advice, supported by high-quality products and distributed by professional, well-educated, ethical, moral advisers. The specific mission should address all of the major financial hazards of living, which I've already stated, but let me re-state them to make the point. Some people are going to die too soon. Many people in today's world are going to live too long. And most people will face unexpected hazards along the way. With proper planning, every one of those risks can be effectively addressed.

In the first three chapters of this book we've talked about the way it was in the last century, a little bit about the way it is today, and with this chapter a wish for some of the things I'd like to see changed in the future.

The rest of the book, and all the subsequent chapters, will involve individual concepts, skill techniques, and ideas that can be implemented today. You, the reader, and all individual practitioners, can utilize the skills and timeless techniques in the subsequent chapters immediately.

The proposed concepts in this chapter will take a while and cannot be done by an individual. If there are going to be changes, there will be changes at the organizational or corporate level and that will take time; but hopefully some of the ideas referred to so far might help open the door to re-evaluation and consideration leading towards another era of Golden Years for the financial advising profession.

Chapter 4

SUCCESS AND LEADERSHIP

Up until this point this book has addressed the big picture, so to speak. It shares some memories of what happened in the last century, what is happening today, and what I personally believe should be different by capturing some of what we've lost of the last century. All of these issues, since they are "big picture items" should be of interest to the reader but have limited, immediate implementation values. I felt, however, that before getting to the specifics for the individual, a broad overview was a solid foundation.

Beginning with this chapter and all of the subsequent chapters, I will be very specific and will address individual skills and techniques, along with concepts, that can be utilized immediately by the individual or reader. Every idea will not be appropriate for every person, but every reader should find among the subsequent concepts and ideas many things that they can utilize to help them achieve even greater success and more happiness.

I have never met a happy failure. Therefore, I have concluded that success is a necessary ingredient for any individual to enjoy total happiness. Before we begin with specific ideas and techniques, we must define success.

Success is, and should be, different for every person. We each have our own dreams and aspirations. If we achieve these goals and concurrently develop great inter-personal relationships with a significant number of people who are important to us, in my mind that person is successful.

However, when we judge success in others, success is usually measured by wealth, position, excellence at a chosen calling, fame, or power.

Of course these two different perceptions are not necessarily mutually exclusive. However, I have known a great many people who are perceived by others to be very successful, but in truth are privately miserable. Wealth often breeds family dysfunction. Power and position often

> Success is usually measured by wealth, position, excellence at a chosen calling, fame, or power.

create jealousy or stress in ones inter-personal relationships. Excellence at a chosen calling sometimes leads to a workaholic obsession and precludes a happy whole life experience. Fame brings with it a fish-bowl type life that many feel overwhelming and, in time, leads to a reclusive life style.

As I have already stated, these reactions to perceived success are not necessarily so, but I don't believe you can be successful by just being so in the eyes of others, you must also be pleased with yourself.

My conclusion therefore, is true and great success is a combination of achieving one's personal dreams and aspirations, enjoying wonderful inter-personal relationships, and then, only if part of your aspirations is to be successful in the eyes of others, concurrently being perceived as successful by whatever criteria people chose to measure you by.

Interestingly, whether we fail, are mediocre, or are successful, in most instances, it is because that is what we chose to be. The few exceptions to this rule are not a product of our own choosing. Some few among us are deprived of the opportunity to control their own destiny. This can be the result of limited physical or mental capacity or perhaps the environment into which we were born. Even with the handicaps there are many who have fought their way to success by sheer courage and determination. Conversely, there are also a lucky few who inherited success or lucked into a windfall that positioned them without their creating the opportunity.

However, for the great, great majority, we ourselves chose to fail, or be mediocre, or succeed, because we each must decide how high a price we are prepared to pay to achieve our dreams and aspirations. It is always easier to fail, or be average, than to really succeed. Hence, the great majorities of people never come close to achieving their potential and live a life of unfulfilled dreams. Classically, these people often blame every one but themselves for their disappointments and frustrations.

It has been said that the difference between successful and unsuccessful people is that the successful people will do the things that unsuccessful people won't do. Please note that I said won't do, not can't do. That is the price of success, and too few people will pay that price.

A good example of a person who wanted to be herself, while concurrently achieving her sense of success, is the story of one of my associates. My phone rang a few years ago and the person on the phone said she would appreciate an appointment to discuss her career opportunities. Of course I agreed and we met. She was a professional looking, charming person and seemed like a good candidate. I asked why she called me, and she said she had already spoken to several other companies in financial services but had heard we were one of the best so she wanted an interview. Also, she had already been turned down by several of the other firms in town, and she was not impressed with the others.

I, as I always do, asked questions to start a relationship, and shut up and listened. She told me straight out that she would only work a four-day week, never on Friday and never on weekends. She further said she wanted at least four two-week vacations every year. I realized that was why the other firms had turned her down, but I was curious as to why she had such strange, and in most instances, unreasonable expectations. It took lots of questions to hear the whole story.

She had been a six-day a week, no vacation time, workaholic in the corporate world, and had achieved lofty titles and high pay. Then, out of the blue, she was diagnosed with advanced breast cancer and needed a double mastectomy; her life was completely shattered. After a long recovery period, she dramatically changed her priorities. Work was no longer primary, but it was still a high priority. She wanted to work with support groups as a volunteer and she wanted to, so to speak, smell the flowers and enjoy life. She believed she could be very successful in an entrepreneurial business working her chosen hours and still live a full and complete life.

I was impressed, but I had to make sure she understood my minimum expectations, measured by performance and production. I also told her I had no problem with whatever work schedule she chose so long as she met our minimum standards. After the usual recruiting and selection process, she joined us as a full time financial advisor.

As she initially stated, she lived rigidly by her work time restrictions. I don't think I ever saw her on a Friday. However with a four-day week and a 44-week year she consistently far exceeded our groups' individual minimums and actually was in the top 20% of our producers every year.

She was a truly happy fulfilled person. She had loads of very special friends and many of them became clients. She played hard, but worked hard as well, and she achieved success as she perceived it, which included the respect and admiration of her clients and peers.

That brings us to what this book is all about. What are the things we must do to be successful?

Of course, the hard way to figure that out is with sheer determination, trial and error techniques, and working intensely for long hours. For those prepared to pay that price, it really works and from this comes some great "Self-Made People."

However, the majority of great successes have accelerated their progress by utilizing mentor relationships, by reading and listening to tapes, by associating with other successful people. Doing so not only makes the road to success much easier, it exploits the wisdom and experiences of those that came before and who have freely shared their story to help others who will follow.

This book includes some of the best information available to show the reader what has to be done to achieve success. It is self evident that conversely it also includes the things that unsuccessful people don't do, hence they never achieve their true potential.

An interesting phenomenon, which is a by-product of success, is one's impact on other people. Negative people often have a negative impact on those around them; yet positive people who have achieved success often positively motivate and inspire other people in their life. All of us have met people who when they enter the room, it's like the sun comes out; the room gets brighter and happier. We've also met people who when they enter the room bring a cloud and dampen the atmosphere because of their negativism.

Even great leaders don't always appreciate how powerful they are in influencing those around them. I learned this lesson a long time ago from a conversation I had with a good friend I mentioned earlier in this book, Tom Wolff. Tom and I were speaking in England, and he was always on one of my favorite people lists. I liked and respected him and recognized him as a great leader in our industry. We never discussed that subject, but one night while in England, I asked him a direct question. "How does it feel to be so respected and be such a powerful leader among our peers in the financial service business?" I was stunned by his answer. He said, with a big smile on his face, "It's funny you should ask me that Norman because for some time I've been wanting to ask you the same thing."

> Even great leaders don't always appreciate how powerful they are in influencing those around them.

Those opening questions led to an in-depth discussion, wherein we both discovered that neither thought of ourselves as powerful leaders or role models, but each had the same perception that the other person was the truly successful leader, and we were the followers. This discovery opened my eyes to a new appreciation and a greater awareness of who the truly successful leaders were in our industry and who was driven by their own ego and personal claim to fame.

The truly successful leader is usually a whole person who enjoys great inter-personal relationships, high family priorities, economic success in the business of their choosing, which then provides the wherewithal of living and providing a wonderful life for those they love.

This has also led to something of a test I use to measure people as leaders and successful individuals. Another incident follows, which helped me understand who the real successes and leaders were that I had the privilege of considering friends.

Most of my career I have been an industry activist but, surprisingly in retrospect, I didn't seek the position. I chose to give of myself to causes I embraced. As a result of this attitude, I had become President of my local Life Underwriters Association, New York City, where I then lived, and that evolved into my going through the Chairs and becoming President of New York State. I had no desire or ambition to go any further.

One day while attending a meeting some very good friends, who were leaders in the New York State association, asked me for some private time to discuss a very important matter. The small group included Al Howes, one of the great life insurance people of all time, Spence McCarty, the executive of the New York State Life Underwriter Association, and Dave Fluegelman, a past National President of the national association who was also from New York.

At this private meeting, they said they would like me to become a candidate to run for the National Board as a representative of our state. Since the thought had never crossed my mind I immediately asked, "Why?" particularly since I knew there was a candidate from upstate New York who had already declared an interest and I presumed would be the New York State candidate. Their explanation was another eye-opener. They said, "Yes, there is a candidate that wants to run, but we're not as concerned with the candidate as we are with the motive." The upstate individual wanted to run for personal ego, status, and position, not in their judgment, to fight for our common cause. They had met separately to figure out who in the state would be an appropriate candidate that they could enthusiastically support.

They decided, though they knew I had no desire or ambition to proceed into the National level, I was the correct candidate, because my commitment was for the well-being of the financial service industry and the success of the industry organizations committed to that cause, not for personal benefit, and not ego-driven.

Initially, reluctantly, but eventually enthusiastically, I pursued that route and eventually became the President of the National Association, but more important at least for me, was the lesson of measuring people by motive and intent, not by their political facade.

The 20th century enjoyed an army of volunteers, some of whom I identified in Chapter 3 of this book as heroes. They gave of themselves freely with no personal motive other than to make this world a better place. I don't think those people, and the many like them I didn't list, should ever be forgotten. They were the mentors and the heroes of the 20th century, and every successful practitioner today has built success on the foundation that these great and successful leaders conceived and created.

Chapter 5

EMPOWERMENT

Without a doubt one of the least understood characteristics of all successful people is what I have come to define as Empowerment. Certainly in the 20th century and, in all likelihood, all of the previous centuries' great successes and leaders had a mysterious strength that, though difficult to define, was very real. It is one of the timeless techniques that every 21st century practitioner should attempt to understand and incorporate in what they do and who they are. Almost every great successful leader I have ever met, in or out of our industry, has this magic and often doesn't even realize it is part of their very being. Other people, however, react to it by giving extra credibility to the empowered few, and they also are inclined to follow their direction and recommendations.

Empowerment has nothing to do with size. In our industry, one of the all time greats is Lyle Blessman. He stands well over six feet tall, has a booming powerful voice, firm handshake, and physically is, in fact, an overwhelming individual. On the other hand, perhaps the greatest financial advisor of all times was Ben Feldman, a short, stocky, soft-spoken individual who even had a slight lisp, but when he whispered people listened, and he had an almost hypnotic impact on everyone he ever met. Both were clearly empowered.

I became very aware that this mystical talent existed because of the part of my career dedicated to recruiting and training individuals. Everyone I ever hired appeared to have the mental and physical capacity to excel in our business. They were all trained with the same materials and taught the same sales procedures. They could deliver a sales presentation exactly the same, word for word, and yet some of those recruits developed into superstars, and others failed dismally and were out of the business in a remarkably short time.

As a manager, I struggled with this problem and came to a couple of early conclusions. One analogy I shared with some of my associates was that I asked them to pretend I was a dance teacher. In a classroom without any music playing, I would do the steps of the fox trot. I would then suggest that every student stand up and do the same step I had just done, counting one. . . two . . .three. . . . It was an easy transition for each student to stand up and replicate the fox trot step one. . .two. .

.three. . . . If at that point I turned on the music for a fox trot and said, "Okay, now each of you get up and dance." They would all without question, be able to do the step, but it wouldn't take an expert choreographer to realize that some of them were truly dancing and some were clumsily getting up and counting one. . .two. . .three. . . . They knew the dance step but they didn't know the music.

I realized that was like teaching someone a sales presentation, where they knew the words but unfortunately, so to speak, they didn't know the music. At my agency meetings during that part of my career, I would invite my legendary friends to come visit and share their expertise. Ben Feldman was one of my invitees, and when he came to the agency, he did a magnificent job sharing some of his perceptions and expertise. He even took questions and one of my associates asked Ben, "Why is it that some people using the same sales presentation consistently strike out, while someone else using that same presentation seemed to consistently make sales?" Ben's answer was classic. He said that people do not necessarily hear the words, they hear you. One salesperson seems to be saying to the prospect, "Mr. Prospect, please buy. I'm desperate, I need a sale. I need the commission. Please buy." And the successful salesperson, though they were using exactly the same words, communicate, "Mr. Prospect, you have a problem and I'm so glad I'm here because when I walk out the door I'm going to take your problem with me, and you're going to be just fine."

From many such instances, I began to realize there was something that they don't teach in class. It's not in any textbooks but there is something special, almost magical, about the super successes in all businesses. That magical skill is what I call Empowerment: The ability to communicate a message that establishes the practitioner as the leader with credibility who other people feel comfortable following. Empowerment.

Once I became aware of this special talent and skill, I had difficulty determining how to transfer that magic to the people I was training and motivating. As a foundation, I remembered from my agricultural and zoological background the psychology of all living beings. As an example, many experiments had been done to establish the existence of what has come to be known as the "pecking order."

The reason for that definition is one of the classic experiments involving chickens. Experimenters discovered that if you put a great number of chickens in an enclosed area and they had never before been together, an amazing thing occurs. At first, what appears to be a raucous fight breaks out. Feathers fly, screaming and clucking dominates the relationships, and then almost miraculously everyone settles down and gets quiet.

However, something has occurred during that initial skirmishing. Every chicken has found out where it fits in the hierarchy of all the other chickens. Somewhere in that group there is a King Chicken that is the most dominant of all and can do anything he or she cares to do. Also in that group, there is a little Chicken Chicken who has been dominated by every other bird in the room and accepts a position of total subservience. When night comes, the King Chicken can roost any place it cares to and the Chicken Chicken will get a last spot down at the bottom of the pile, where all the other bird's droppings may be hitting it all night long, but that is its fate because of pecking order relationships. Every bird fits in the hierarchy from the most dominant to the most submissive.

This trait is not unique with chickens. Almost all animals accept their position in the hierarchy of life, and this is usually established without any blood spilled, though often in the choosing of sides, it looks like there will be some physical damage done, but rarely does that actually happen.

The human being is not that different. I would go out on interviews with one of my associates to observe their sales skills. If the prospect was a personal friend, approximately the same age and in approximately the same financial situation, the interview might go something like this.

"Hi John. Great seeing you. There's something I'd like to show you that I know will be of great personal value. Why don't you pull over a chair and let me show you one of the greatest things I've ever seen that I think would be perfect for you." On another interview, sometimes immediately following the one I just described, the salesperson might be calling on a friend of his father who is significantly older, substantially richer, and the leader of a company. The same agent would conduct an interview that would begin something like this. "Uhhh, Mr. Smith thank you for seeing me. I really appreciate your giving me some of your time. I know you're a good friend of my father and there is something I'd like to show you that you might find interesting, or if you can spare a few moments, I'd like to show it to you but, would it be all right if I sit in the chair by your desk?"

What happened between those two interviews? Actually, nothing. In the first interview, in their pecking order relationship, my salesman associate was a King Chicken. In the second interview, only in his or her own mind, the salesperson was a Chicken Chicken. Unless the friend of the father wanted to do a favor for his friends' son, he wouldn't buy, while the first interview certainly could lead to a potential sale.

What I've already discussed in this chapter is the background for development of an awareness that empowerment comes from four attributes that the King Chicken always has. The good news is I have learned by developing these skills, empowerment can be developed.

To help my associates understand empowerment and the four attributes, I use an acronym to remind them of each of the four principles. The acronym is BEAK. The beak is the most powerful part of the symbol of our great country, the eagle. It is also the key to the strength leaders.

B stands for Belief. That sounds simple, but it really isn't. I have met financial advisors who are embarrassed about being a commission-based salesperson and who feel inferior to their professional friends. They are afraid of requesting action from a

B stands
for Belief.

potential prospect, they lack personal self-confidence, they don't necessarily believe in themselves and what they're doing, or the fantastic profession we represent. They might say otherwise, but when I have a chance to dig deep into their thinking, some grown human beings have actually broken down and cried in my presence because of the embarrassment and shame of what they perceive to be their greatest weakness. Addressing Belief is critical to great success.

Often, people I am working with say, "But I don't know what I really believe," or, "I have no absolute strong beliefs." Sixty years of working with other people have convinced me that is never the case. Everyone has beliefs. They may not be consistent with success, but they heavily influence everything they do.

The analogy I often use to make this point is kind of silly, but in its own strange way, powerful. I love Broadway shows. I see every show I can possibly see, many of them many times. One of my favorites has always been Peter Pan. Though it's often perceived to be a kid's show, I find it delightful and entertaining. There is one segment of Peter Pan, however, that I have often used to explain Belief in a way many of my associates had not previously understood.

Peter Pan is a young boy who refuses to grow up and has an amazing talent. He can fly. He has one really good friend, Tinkerbell. Tinkerbell is a fairy. In the stage shows you never really see Tinkerbell, but you always know when Tinkerbell is there because Tinkerbell is represented by a little light that blinks on and off and beeps as it goes. Tinkerbell is very fond of Peter Pan and at this point in the show is aware that the pirates are going to poison Peter Pan. Tinkerbell gets very agitated and starts beeping and blinking intensely. Peter Pan understands Tinkerbell and says, "That's ridiculous, the pirates aren't going to poison me," and is about to actually drink the poison. Tinkerbell, out of frustration, finally gives up, jumps into the glass and drinks all the poison. Almost immediately the light begins to blink less frequently and dimmer and the beeps get weaker and weaker.

Peter Pan realizes it really was poison and his good friend, Tinkerbell, has sacrificed his life to save him. But then Peter Pan looks out into the audience, which always has a large number of children among the attendees, and says, "Oh my God, it was poison, but we can save Tinkerbell. We can save Tinkerbell if we let Tinkerbell know that we believe in fairies. Do you believe in fairies?"

At first no one in the audience responds. But Peter Pan again says, "Tinkerbell is going to die unless you believe in fairies! Do you believe in fairies? Let me hear you!" Uusually somewhere in the audience one little voice shouts out "I believe!" And Peter Pan looks out at the audience and says, "That's good, but that's not enough, you *all* must believe. Do you believe in fairies?" Almost every time, everyone in the audience starts screaming "I believe, I believe!" Some of the children actually jump on their chairs waving their hands, "I believe, I believe!" Suddenly Tinkerbell's light begins to blink again, brighter and brighter and the beeping gets louder and louder, and Tinkerbell is back.

Now at first when I saw that, it was just a silly children's story. Kids believe in the Easter Bunny, Santa Claus, fairies, and Peter Pan, but we adults are too mature for that. But are we? Sure we outgrow tooth fairies and Santa Claus, but do each of us have things we believe, right to our very core, that we cannot scientifically prove or logically and objectively confirm, but we know it's true? Who among us doesn't have some beliefs that can never be shaken? Love, faith, country, friends, and so much more. We know that we'd have a hard time proving that those beliefs are real. Our successful leaders have similar beliefs but, without exception, they also believe in themselves. They believe in what they're doing and in our business. They believe in the miracle we carry in our attaché case. They know people aren't doing them a favor when they buy. They are doing them a favor by helping them address their wants and aspirations.

Belief, the first letter of BEAK is the foundation of empowerment, but it must be accompanied by the other three attributes. The letter "E" represents Enthusiasm. I have never met an enthusiastic loser. All of the empowered people I know are enthusiastic.

> The letter "E" represents Enthusiasm.

Early in my career, I was encouraged to read Frank Bettger's book, *How I Raised Myself From Failure to Success*. I eventually got to know Frank. I heard him speak and was on the same program with him on a couple of occasions, and he was truly an extraordinary man. He had been a baseball player, came into our business, and became a super-star as an insurance salesperson. However, the bottom line of his sales skill was his capacity to utilize one basic truth: *Before you can become something, you must act that way.* People want to do business with successful people, and people want to do business with winners, not losers. The ability to communicate with enthusiasm is the secret of developing an image that prospects and friends learn to respect and admire.

In the specifics of enthusiasm Frank said, "If you want to be enthusiastic, you might not always feel enthusiastic, but without any question you must always *act* enthusiastic. You must *act* enthusiastic to *be* enthusiastic." I've done that all my life and, then, one day I woke up and realized I wasn't acting anymore. I am an extremely positive, enthusiastic person and it began with the basic concept – you must *act* to *be*.

A good friend of mine, one of the super-star legends in our industry, and I heard Frank Bettger speak in the first few years of our career. Frank gave a great speech at a company meeting and that night he was sitting in the lobby of the hotel holding court with those of us who sat at his feet to pick his brains and learn some of the magic. My good friend, and eventual super-star, had been working on the biggest case he had ever tried to sell in his life, and up until that point in time, had failed miserably. He asked Frank Bettger what he could do to sell the case, and he described the case to Frank. All of us expected a technical answer. Frank's response was very dramatic. He said, "Young man, didn't you hear me speak this morning?" My friend said, "Yes, of course." Frank said, "What did you hear me say?" And my good friend said, "Lots of things." But Frank then said, "Wasn't there a basic, primary principle?" My friend said, "I'm not quite sure what you mean." Frank Bettger said, "Watch me."

We were in a conservative, staid, old New England hotel with a significant number of guests that had nothing to do with our meeting. Frank Bettger got up in the lobby and went storming around the lobby, screaming at the top of his lungs, "You've got to *act* enthusiastic to *be* enthusiastic!" Each time he slammed his hands together, and then again took a couple of steps screaming, "You've got to *act* enthusiastic to *be* enthusiastic!"

When he had made a complete circle of the lobby with most of the guests looking at him like he was out of his mind, he sat down and said, "Young man, do you now understand?" My friend, who was thoroughly cowed (talk about pecking-order relationships), said, "Yes sir!", and didn't intend to pursue the matter. However, Frank Bettger said, "Okay, if you mean that, now you get up and do what I just did." This young man, in his 20s, just barely in the business, got up in front of not only our group, but all of the non-meeting guests, and went storming around the lobby screaming, "You've got to *act* enthusiastic to *be* enthusiastic!"

The case, as to the specifics, was never discussed. My friend told me an amazing story. After that meeting he arranged another appointment with the prospects who until that point in time had turned him down on every visit. On the way to the prospects business, my friend stopped in a wood lot and went out by himself in the wood lot, screaming at the top of his lungs, "You've got to *act* enthusiastic to *be* enthusiastic!" He got his adrenaline flowing and then went to see the prospects with exactly the same presentation he had given in his previous efforts. Only this time he was charged. He closed the case, the largest case he had ever written, solely on the emotion of "You've got to *act* enthusiastic to *be* enthusiastic!"

How do people perceive you? Are you smiling or frowning? Are you enthusiastic or passive? Enthusiasm requires an active attitude, not just on sales interviews, but all-day every-day. It's a discipline that, as Frank Bettger said a lot of years ago, "You've got to *act* that way to *be* that way," until it becomes you. I respectfully suggest if you're not already totally enthusiastic, it's worth working on that skill.

The third letter "A" represents Activity. That's more relevant in our business than in many other businesses because part of empowerment reflects the desperation of having to make a sale, as opposed to the luxury of having more people to see than you have time to see.

The third letter "A" represents Activity.

Part of Empowerment is strictly a matter of Activity. In the 20th century, seeing 15 people a week and making at least one or two sales a week was an expected minimum. Accountability meant those targets couldn't be ignored and, though everyone didn't attain them every week, it was an honest target for everybody.

The Million Dollar Round Table's average member sells well over 100 sales a year, which obviously is more than two a week. Some of the top producers sell almost 10 a week. When a financial advisor in the formative stages sees only two or three people a week, it is obvious that they are going to be in trouble building their career.

Empowerment in part is being aware you have lots of people to see and they're not doing you a favor, you're doing a service for their best interests. Later on in Chapter Nine entitled "Seeing People," I will spend significant time on how one can go about significantly increasing their level of activity and to do it in a way that is both fun and profitable.

The last letter in the acronym for Empowerment is "K" which stands for Knowledge. Obviously, this book cannot include educational material that can better be provided by the CLU, ChFC, CFP, and LUTCF programs, and so many more that are easily available. The point here under Empowerment, however, is one's confidence and therefore, Empowerment is directly related to one's own comfort level and self-confidence in addressing the wants and needs of prospects. Lack of education, and therefore knowledge, will also result in a lack of the feeling of empowerment. The less secure a financial advisor is in his or her ability to respond to the problems of the potential client, the less the level of Empowerment. It is okay to say "I don't know, but I will get you the answer," but not all the time. The financial advisor should be well-educated with a pool of knowledge that gives him or her a sense of empowerment and self-confidence to meet with any prospect, any time, any place.

"K" stands for Knowledge.

I strongly recommend that the reader who is not certain they have developed the 'pecking-order' skills of Empowerment spend time every week building their confidence with education, increased activity, *acting* enthusiastic to *be* enthusiastic, and reaffirming their belief in what they're doing and who they are.

Chapter 6

BUILDING TRUSTING RELATIONSHIPS

One of the primary themes of this book is that some things never change and are just as important in the 21st century as they have been historically. There is no better example then the building of trusting relationships as the foundation of both good social and business activities. The problem is we were trained for trusting relationships in the last century, and it is a neglected skill in today's limited training environment. Trusting relationships, however, are not a reflection of what one does when they are working, but rather how they are perceived as a whole person. To build a strong trusting image is a 24-hour-a-day, seven-day-a-week project. It is how you live and how you interrelate with all of the people, all of the time. In my training and coaching experience, it quickly became evident that no matter what façade an individual tries to build around their personal image, the great majority of people see them as they really are.

I once did an experiment with a group I was training. I first asked each one to write a description of how they thought they were perceived. Almost without exception each person had a lofty impression of themselves. However, I then asked each person in the room, using just a few adjectives, to describe every other person in the room as they perceived them. The first revelation was that a significant number of attendees, lofty self-impressions notwithstanding, were perceived by their peer group to have many personality flaws. There were, of course, some whose self-perception and the perception of their peers were almost identical. But there is no question that regardless of one's attempt to impress others, in time, everyone figures out the truth about each of us.

> In time, everyone figures out the truth about each of us.

It appears some people knowingly lied about their own trusting image, but others believe their self-analysis, because they presumed they had done an effective "con job" on the people with whom they interrelated. Nonetheless, it is very apparent that most people can accurately recognize the real personality of other people. Most importantly, that includes the attributes of trust and dependability that most people seek in their friends and business advisors. Once that became apparent, as part of my business coaching and training, I had to incorporate "building trusting relationship" into my training procedures.

I frequently use acronyms, as you read in the last chapter when we discussed BEAK and empowerment, and I am about to introduce you to another acronym as it relates to trusting relationships. The reason I use acronyms is that in training people, where there are multiple issues pertaining to that particular subject, I find that people remember the component parts more easily if they know the acronym, which helps them recall the multiple issues.

The acronym for trusting relationships is "WINE CASK." Each letter represents one of the eight attributes I have found to be essential for a person to build a trusting image leading to trusting relationships. Remember, we are talking about seven days a week, 24 hours a day, not just work time, as we each are perceived as a whole person. It is on that overall perception that judgments are determined. I strongly recommend the reader test him- or herself against each of these attributes because even one weak spot will impact your total image.

W   Work ethic is a critical component. Are you dependable? Always on time or early? Or are you someone that people get to expect to be late or even worse, not to be there at all? Are you the first person in the office in the morning and last one to leave at night, or last one in the morning and first one out at night? Work ethic reflects dependability. Can people count on you? Would you want to do financial business with someone you couldn't depend on and who was clearly lazy in their work disciplines? If you go to a place of business that is supposed to open at 8:00 a.m. and you arrive after 8:00 a.m., and the doors are still locked, will you ever go back to that business again? A retail business might survive such an experience, but financial advisors are individuals, and the lack of dependability always will open the door to competition.

I   Involvement. Are you a recluse or a good citizen in the community and within your profession? Are you active in charities, social activities, local politics, business trade associations, etc. Obviously, you don't have to be intensely involved in all of these persuasions, but you certainly ought to be visible in some of them. As an example, friends and clients frequently call me for what they perceive to be a favor – tickets for some show that were unavailable to the public, membership in some special clubs, the purchase of some high cost item, or whatever. I am not a power broker in my own right, but because of my heavy involvement in multiple activities within the community, I knew the people who were. I could get favors done for the people in my world by asking the right people, who because of our mutual involvements were happy to help. As an example, I had six tickets for what were known to be the best seats in the house, those normally reserved for theater critics, for every Broadway show that came to San Francisco in all of the theaters. I had tickets in the second row on the center isle for the San Francisco Opera opening night series. I had six tickets on the 50-yard line for the San Francisco 49ers when they were almost impossible to get. I also had six tickets for the Raiders, also on the 50-yard line. When I moved to San Francisco in 1974-1975 all of those tickets, and the membership in some of the more illustrious clubs, had long waiting lists and were not available. In a relatively short time, I met the people who helped make them available, and eventually I had the tickets and membership in three very special clubs. Incidentally, the reason I always got six tickets was it gave me an opportunity; as a matter of fact it almost forced me, to invite two other couples to join me on each of these occasions. This was usually preceded by dinner or a luncheon and always hosted by me. The guests could have been business associates, clients, or friends. When I invited them and they were not available, it still scored points with the invitee, and I often got positive recognition from more people than the actual ticket count. I quickly got to know the right people while doing a good deed for the community, by being involved in professional, philanthropic, political, and cultural groups. I strongly suggest you find causes in which you believe, join a supporting organization, and then take an active position in those organizations.

N No Broken Promises. Trust presumes you will deliver. Anytime you have made a commitment to an individual, whether they are a prospect, client, or friend, you must deliver on schedule, but preferably ahead of schedule. If you say something will be done on Tuesday, have it done on Monday. If Tuesday comes and it is not done, don't hope they won't notice, but pick up the phone and explain why the delay and promise to get back to them by a certain time, which you will then try actively to exceed.

> If you say something will be done on Tuesday, have it done on Monday.

E Ethics and Morality. Every one of the eight attributes that have been identified by WINE CASK are important, but this one is more than just absolute and must be rigidly embraced. No matter how good a job you do in relationships with people, even over a long period of time, one transgression will undo everything you have ever achieved. The problem is there are a lot of gray areas. Of course, there is a right and a wrong, a legal and an illegal, but an awful lot of things fall in the cracks between the two. The smart practitioner stays safely out of the gray areas and lives by the absolute right and legal. I have been called square, and probably have lost potential clients because of my rigidity in this area. On the other hand, I have never been sued, nor can I ever remember losing a client because I did something wrong. When an associate in my organization came to me and would begin the discussion with a question that went something like this: Would it be okay if I did such and such? My answer was always, if there is enough of a doubt for you to ask the question, don't do it. It may be legal and it may even, on analysis, be right, but if there is enough of a doubt for you to ask the question, others will do the same. So don't do it. You can't be half pregnant and you can't be half honest. You either are or you are not. As I have suggested to my associates and have realized in my own career, by being square and straight, I have occasionally lost a potential client, but in the long run, because of my devotion, commitment, and loyalty to my clients and of my clientele back to me, I have significantly exceeded those losses with more new clients, new business, and the respect of my peers. Also very important, I sleep well at night.

C Compassion. One of the books I previously wrote was entitled *Passion for Compassion*. I felt that was the shortest possible definition of the perfect financial advising practitioner. Passion was the way of saying the practitioner had a fire in their belly that created a commitment to the work they were doing and provided the discipline to implement the methodology to be among the best. Compassion means the work and discipline was not for the commissions or the sales, but rather their caring for other people and helping them to achieve their dreams and aspirations. When a person thinks you are primarily motivated by what's in it for yourself, they will never completely trust you. On the other hand, when that same person believes they have found someone who really cares about them and is dedicated to helping them achieve their life's desires, the foundation of a great trusting relationship has been established.

A Attitude. No one likes to be surrounded by negativity. A good friend of mine, who is now a super star in our industry, told me that he announced he was quitting the business six times before he finally made it. He has now been in the business for over 50 years. When I asked him what made the difference, he said he was in an agency where most of the other new people, and even some of the hanger-on older more experienced folks, would get together for lunch or coffee sometime during the day.

No one likes to be surrounded by negativity.

The conversation always turned out to be a contest for who was suffering the most. Who hadn't made a sale? Who had made a sale and lost it? Who had clients who had changed their mind and backed out of a deal? It became a one-upmanship contest for failures. My friend was struggling like everyone else and was often depressed and moody during those early years. But his feelings were compounded by the negativism of the group with whom he had been associating. He finally dropped out of the group when one of the older more successful agents in his agency befriended him and became, in effect, his unofficial mentor. He did joint work with him, boosted his morale, motivated him to raise his sights, and inevitably my friend began to do better and better and better.

I had a similar experience that related to my management activities. As you know by now, I was a long-time significant personal producer, but I also was a general agent running a fairly large financial advising organization. That never would have happened if not for a very good friend who happened to be the Vice President of the company I then represented. The company asked me to go into management and start a new agency, which I decided to do. However, after a couple of years I was utterly frustrated. I was associating with the leaders of other agencies within the company who were also relatively new, and whose organizations were quite small. Their producers were doing very little business and the overall feeling was that we were not building the highly successful, high-income organization I aspired to create. I told my Vice President friend, Roe Maier, I wanted to resign from management and I explained why. We were good friends, and he suggested I come up to his home near our home office in Hartford, Connecticut because he had an idea that might help me reevaluate my decision. I was excited to do so, and I arrived on a Sunday, planning to stay an entire week. Monday morning Roe took me to see a friend of his, Harold Smyth, who was the head of a very successful financial organization representing a competing company, National Life of Vermont. Roe had arranged for me to spend a week with Harold and observe how he went about running his agency, and each night I returned to Roe's home where we enjoyed dinner and a discussion of what management could be. At the end of that week I was totally recommitted to management, but with a whole new perspective as to what the challenge really meant. As a result, I went back to my agency and totally restructured the organization, changed my recruiting and selection standards, built in new training methodologies, and set minimum expectations that far exceeded my original plan. As I've already stated, my agency rose to the number one life insurance agency in the company, and we had more million dollar round table producers than any other agency in the company. That was the beginning of what eventually evolved into the Levine Financial Group. Attitude is a critical component for trust. There was an agent in my agency that my associates named Dr. Doom. He always knew why everything would not work. He believed he was objective and positive, but his peers knew the truth. He never fit the agency and was gone in a very short time. You must associate with winners and dream dreams to be a winner. We are each in this way missionaries carrying a message of positive fulfillment and excitement, or one of negative poison and under achieving. To be trusted, you must be perceived as a positive person and a winner.

S Skills, but most particularly people skills. It is not closing techniques and answering objections that are the key to the skills that make one a successful practitioner. It is the ability to interrelate with people and get their confidence and their loyalty. Interpersonal skills are an almost lost art. The outstanding retail organizations, the better restaurants, the finest hotels clearly stand apart because of the discipline and training their employees get to make the customer feel important and well served. In none of those professions are people skills more important than in financial advising. People reluctantly go for annual physical checkups and, with even less enthusiasm, see the dentist regularly. But many don't. Even those that do are not enthused at the anticipation of those visits. Dying too soon, outliving your money because you live too long, or the hazards that can happen along the way are certainly not the highlight of anyone's life, but they are real and someone must make every individual face that reality. As has already been stated, part of it is the overall trusting relationship, but a significant part of it is the skill of the practitioner in getting the prospect or client to face the unpleasantness of life's hazards. This is an art form that is rarely, if ever, taught. It requires practice, practice, practice. My school for learning this skill was probably my Fuller-Brush experience, of seeing hundreds of people a week and learning how to communicate effectively and develop trusting relationships. Some people are blessed with a natural gift in this area, but most have to learn it to be interpersonally effective. There will be many ideas shared in the balance of this book that will contribute towards growth in this area, but in reality the only school that I have personally seen that has been effective in developing interpersonal skills is the school of experience. When a practitioner only sees two or three people a week, and is desperate to do business, it is impossible to hone the interpersonal skill.

In Chapter 9, Seeing People, I will share a people skill technique I call the "non-interview," which should help master this skill. Involvement and company activities, seeing lots of people at least socially, if not for business, and learning to communicate will in time sharpen one's interpersonal people skills. In some ways this skill is a little bit of show business. An introvert with a poor personality might very well be a loving, caring, sharing individual, but the new acquaintance or prospect, except perhaps for their closest friends, is unaware of his internal charm. Practitioners in financial advising have very little time to make that important first impression, and regardless of the internal motivation and sincere commitment, it is important to develop the charm, the smooth communication skills necessary to be an affective people person.

K Knowledge. This was also in the BEAK acronym in the last chapter. As I suggested then, this book cannot be a financial advisor textbook providing a full education. This must be attained elsewhere. However, in the context of trust, knowledge is essential. You should be able to communicate, not just on subjects relating to financial advising, but on all areas of human interest. Without knowledge, as perceived by your constituencies, you will never have a complete trusting relationship. On the other hand, nobody can know everything about everything. If a relevant issue is raised, and you do not know the answer, simply suggest "I don't know, but I will find out and let you know by next Tuesday." Then call with the answer by Monday. You can't always say I don't know, but people understand when it happens occasionally. That is why we all need continuing education and some truly professional degrees, and the appropriate letters after your name advertises your credentials and knowledge.

> Without knowledge you will never have a complete trusting relationship.

So that's the acronym – **WINE CASK.** Work ethic, involvement, no broken promises, ethics, compassion, attitude, skills, particularly people skills, and knowledge. As I said at the outset of this chapter, these are the attributes against which we are all measured. It isn't just our work periods that determine people's perception of who we are and what we do. It is the way we act every waking minute of every day. To discipline ones self, to incorporate these eight attributes into our family life, our community activities, our professional practicing, are the secrets of building a permanent image of personal trust and thereby building trusting relationships.

Chapter 7

THE EVOLUTION OF FINANCIAL ADVISING

The evolution of financial advising sounds historical and academic, but it is one of the keys to the development of financial advisors. What we now know as an advisor transitioned differently in each of the financial persuasions. As I have already indicated in previous parts of this book, banking, the investment business, property and casualty insurance brokers, and life insurance agents have all been in transition for several decades. Though each began as specialists, they are all evolving towards the same diversified professional, a totally qualified and well-educated financial advisor. The significance of that phenomenon is that all the different persuasions will now have similar portfolios, and they all will be attempting to serve the same clientele. The difference will no longer be product-based, but will be a direct reflection of the practitioner's skill and knowledge. A perfect example of this movement towards a common end can be found in my good friend and the co-author of one of my earlier books, Bill Bachrach.

Bill's introduction into financial services was as an investment advisor. That was his specialty, and in fact, he excelled. He became aware that the future would require embracing a totally diversified portfolio represented by a qualified total financial advisor. He went on to create the concept of value-based selling, which presumed the development of trusted financial advisors, and he developed a complete program for these future advisors. He built an organization to develop and market the materials to train and educate future financial advisors. He ran academies and wrote books, and he and I, as good friends, began to realize that I was following the same road coming from a life insurance specialization. The Levine Financial Group was also producing total financial advisors. We were recruiting and training candidates into a financial advisor program within my organization. So both of us, once specialists from different backgrounds, evolved into developing similar financial service professionals for the future.

In our relationship, we co-authored a book for managers entitled *High Trust Leadership*. I have attended and spoken at Bill's academies, and he has frequently visited my world.

When I coach aspiring financial advisors, some of whom are already quite successful, I start with the premise that we are going to address three questions in order to accomplish three basic objectives. First, what are they now doing that they shouldn't be doing? Second, what are they not doing that they should be doing? And, third, whatever they should be doing, can they do it better? This book is filled with ideas and concepts that might suggest to the reader that there are things that they are now doing that would be better delegated or eliminated. There are things they are not doing that they should immediately embrace in their daily business practices. And third, very possibly, there are things they are now doing, that they should be doing, that could be done better.

The evolution of the financial advisor is one of the sources to help decide what to do in order to be more effective in the future. The reason I say that is because in my training and speaking activities, I constantly run into large numbers of so-called advisors, matured professional advisors, who are still practicing as if they were in the early stages of the evolutionary process I'm about to describe. You don't become a financial advisor by simply changing your name. Product pushers and pure sales people are, in most instances, unqualified and undisciplined in the profession of totally diversified trusted financial advisors.

I've lived through the evolution I am about to describe. For the younger reader, you might find it interesting. Since all the financial persuasions seem to be moving toward the same ultimate goal, I will only describe the evolutionary process that I lived through as a life insurance producer, but the evolutionary concepts are applicable to all of the different financial persuasions.

For most of the 20th century, life insurance agents were pure product pushers. As I suggested earlier, some carried coffins and little gadgets to get the attention of the prospect and, verbally, would all but backup the hearse. Need selling had not yet been conceived and fear was one of the primary motivators to making a sale. In effect, the life insurance agent would say, "You are going to die," or "You are going to be impoverished if you are blessed with longevity and reach retirement."

> For most of the 20th century, life insurance agents were pure product pushers.

That type of selling slowly was replaced by "need selling." The salesmen would talk about what they perceived the prospect needed, and regardless of that perceived need, since they only had one product in their portfolio, the solution was always *life insurance*.

Then came a somewhat more sophisticated approach to need selling. The sales person would discuss multiple needs, again, as he perceived them, such as dying too soon, children's education, mortgages, living too long, economic and physical hazards along the way, etc. Once the prospect showed concern and interest, the salesman would then again sell the only product in their portfolio, as the solution for all their different needs: *life insurance*. This method of selling was called programming and was extensively used after World War II and well into the 60's.

Larry Wilson developed an organization that many companies used to help train their producers. He developed a somewhat more sophisticated technique than simple programming and called it "consultative selling." The trainee was taught to show compassion, listen more and speak less, and then, in effect, make recommendations. It really was not unlike programming, and the solution was always the only solution that could be sold by a life insurance professional: *life insurance*. The same medicine for every disease.

By the 70's a few pioneers, of which I'm proud to be one, began to do true advisor type selling. This had been impossible until we were able to diversify our portfolio to include all financial products. We could then be totally objective and recommend a program utilizing the appropriate product for the appropriate problem.

I lived and worked through that entire evolution, though in retrospect, in my early career, I was selling over-priced and only partially appropriate products. However, I have no guilt because I know every person who followed my recommendations was better off financially for that decision, and in those days there were no other options. What we achieved for our clients could not have been accomplished any other way. With each evolutionary step I, and my peers, matured and quickly embraced change in order to be a more professional practitioner.

By the 1970's, I had created a completely operational, full-service, totally diversified, financial service organization. All of our representatives were trained and educated in the skills of true financial advisors. One of my frustrations, even today, are the majority of people I meet professing to be professional advisors are still actually selling by utilizing one of the middle stages of the evolutionary process I just described.

There are some key differences between selling and advising, which quickly show me the level of competence of a professed advisor.

Four of the key attributes of the advisor as opposed to the sales person are as follows:

The salesman sells *need* as they perceive the problem. The advisor finds out what the prospect *wants* to accomplish and helps them achieve it using the appropriate vehicles to get there.

The salesman has a sales track and *talks*, and talks, and talks some more. The advisor *asks questions* and *listens*.

The sales person talks about *products*, how good they are and what they cost. The advisor, after listening to find out what people want, proposes *solutions* for the prospects' problems.

> The advisor asks questions and listens.

And finally, the sales person is often *high tech*, but the advisor is *high touch* and spends considerable time establishing strong interpersonal relationships.

As the basis of all advisor relationships and recommendations, the advisor always gets a fact finder or data sheet. The sales person may or may not always use that procedure.

This has been an overview description of the "evolution" in the life insurance industry. All the other financial specialties were concurrently evolving to provide their clients with diversified financial advisors.

You might ask, "Who needs a financial advisor?" By some people's implications, only the wealthy require financial advice and justify the time and attention of a trusted financial advisor. That is because there is a perception in the industry that the true financial advisor is an elitist and only serves the wealthy. A few people hunting in a very limited market. Of course, there is some truth to that perception because of the way the concept of the financial advisor is promoted, but I don't agree with that premise. Not only don't I agree with that premise, I believe it is counterproductive to what should be our industry's mission. Our industry should be committed to helping all our citizens solve the very serious and real problems of living too long, dying too soon, and the economic and physical hazards that occur along the way.

The elitist attitudes have the great majority of fully qualified financial advisors serving only the wealthy and the upper middle class, and by so doing, neglecting the great majority of consumers. Even the product pushers in our industry are neglecting a very large percentage of the consuming public. This vacuum could eventually impact the viability of our industry as the free enterprise provider of financial security for our society. If that were to happen, some alternative would be considered and I fear that might be the government. The point is we must do a better job serving the masses by finding ways to provide the proper advice and financial services for a significantly larger percentage of the population.

To make the point, let's take a look at the situation from a market place perspective. Though it is an over-simplistic approach, we can divide society into three economic groups: the wealthy, including the upper middle class; the rest of the middle class, including the marginal poor; and the poverty level. Financial advisors have concentrated their effort on the top group. I confess my personal market, after I matured in this business, has also been in that market. However, my agency, which was built on brand new recruits served the wealthy, as well as the middle-income markets, and often the lowest income group. These were fully trained financial advisors with a complete diversified portfolio, but they did not only target the upscale market.

We can divide society into three economic groups.

Some of our elitist competitors suggested we were using an elephant gun on mice, but I disagree. Of course, the lower the prospect's income the lower the need for long and complicated, sophisticated solutions. Also, the sales were completed in less time, but usually for smaller volumes and smaller annual deposits. However, the prospects got the kind of qualified advice they really needed.

Let me ask a few questions that will also make the point. Which economic group is most likely to be severely economically disadvantaged by a premature death? Which by a disabling injury? Which by job loss because of a company downsizing? Which by enjoying extended life after retirement?

In my opinion, the wealthiest can survive all of the above without a financial advisor. That was my market, but frankly I helped with their taxes, their corporate needs, and their estate transfer problems; but even without my help they were not facing catastrophic problems. Of course, I am proud of what I accomplished in those areas. I am sure I have saved many businesses, helped keep jobs for people, saved lots of potential unnecessary taxes, avoided in-fighting between beneficiaries after client deaths, etc. However, I can remember Larry Wilson preaching about the difference between an inconvenience and a catastrophe, and in proper objective perspective, my really wealthy clients were never personally at risk for a catastrophe but at the worst, faced some potential inconveniences.

However, the middle group and lower group, which constitute the great majority of the population, are very vulnerable to catastrophic harm in all the areas those questions addressed. Early death often leaves widows and orphans without the financial resources to provide a life with dignity. Elderly people that retire without adequate planning often end up in institutions where the smell of urine and the indignities of public healthcare are overwhelming, and for all people without wealth, a long disability often leads to a frightful life of despair. Those are really catastrophes.

I wish there was some practical way to assist the poverty group, but I suspect government programs were intended to ease their pain and needs because in reality they do not have the resources to do it themselves. But politics aside, in our great country they represent a very small percentage of the population in comparison to the rest of the nations in this world. It is not for the lack of compassion that I recognize the private sector and financial advisors have very limited value in that marketplace.

It seems to me, however, that any family that has a proper dwelling, a car, and at least one person, probably two, gainfully employed deserves a practitioner that teaches, preaches, and provides the programs that secure their well being in all the scenarios mentioned above.

Can you make more money and get away with seeing fewer people in the affluent market place? Of course you can. However, a financial advisor primarily working the middle income market can more easily see more people in the same amount of time, make more and easier sales, and, most importantly, really make a major difference in people's lives when bad things happen.

On the chance that there is some misunderstanding as to what I mean when I say "Financial Advisor," let me clarify my thinking. Certainly the fee based advisor who receives a fee for doing financial plans qualifies. Also, the more sophisticated upscale market professional that, though working for commissions, does total planning, encompassing all available investment and insurance products qualifies.

However, the practitioners that we as an industry need as a qualified financial advisor are the masses of professionals with diversified portfolios contacting, as prospects, the middle class population.

The bottom line? Let me suggest that financial advising is not elitist and superior, it is not exclusively for the wealthy, and it is not a mystique to be learned and practiced by a few. I believe with convergence, with the diversified portfolios available to all practitioners, and with the tremendous untapped market in the middle income group, that every current and future insurance and investment licensee should learn and practice the skills of the total "Trusted Financial Advisor" and apply them to every existing client and future prospect.

Chapter 8

CONVERGENCE

As I suggested in the last chapter, most financial service practitioners, and the companies and firms they represent, are embracing total financial service advisors as their marketing representatives. In time, as the different institutions achieve success, the practitioners representing all of the different companies will, in effect, be doing the same thing with similar diversified product portfolios.

I came to the conclusion that this was the appropriate methodology for properly serving the consumer almost 50 years ago. I had been frustrated by my inability to properly provide security for my personal clients in the three inevitable risk areas – dying too soon, living too long, and the hazards along the way. I wasn't sure how to address that problem, but I was looking for an answer when I had the good fortune to read the results of a research project that the Stanford Research Institute (SRI) had done, I believe for the banking industry, in the late 60's. That research concluded that the typical consumer really wanted an advisor who was a high touch, caring person and was competent to give financial advice embracing all aspects of the financial portfolio. The consumer wanted one individual who was primarily concerned with the consumer's well being. SRI further suggested it was unlikely that any one individual could be a true expert in each of the different financial persuasions. However, they believed this high touch individual could certainly provide the interpersonal relationship that consumers sought. The question of where to get the expertise was also considered, and SRI thought the answer was that the organization that the individual practitioners represented could provide a team of professional experts covering the entire gamut of financial products and services. The high touch person could utilize this expertise and provide the consumer with both high tech and high touch.

Once I read that survey, I realized here is the key for what would eventually become the Levine Financial Group. I decided I would shift my recruiting to finding high touch individuals who had the passion to help people solve their financial problems and to provide security for their loved ones. I also decided it was necessary to concurrently build a support organization, including specialists in every persuasion, to help the financial advisor create and implement programs designed to help consumers achieve their dreams and aspirations. At that time there were few, if any, financial institutions that embraced all of the different product lines and also provided the expertise and services for the field practitioner. Therefore, at my own expense, and using trial and error methodology, which sometimes worked and sometimes didn't, I built the Levine Financial Group. In time we worked out the bugs and, in some instances, we had to restart different specialties several times. We eventually ended up with a complete financial service organization.

I didn't realize that what I was doing would eventually be provided at no cost by different financial institutions. To illustrate to the consumer what the Levine Financial Group was doing, I created a wheel (see Figure 8.1) explaining that the Levine Financial Group high touch representative was at the hub of the wheel, and each of the spokes included products and services that we made available to our financial advisors to help solve their clients' financial problems. Though in time all the major financial institutions included all of those products in their portfolio, for some years our firm had a near exclusive methodology and product line.

Figure 8.1

Besides the wheel, which was an easy way of explaining the many products and services our organization had available to our prospects and clients, it was also apparent that our sales representatives, who were being trained to transition to total financial advising, needed to understand how to utilize all of those products and to build financial plans for their prospects and clients. They also needed a simple uncomplicated one-pager to accompany the wheel, in order to explain how our diversified portfolio would help a client attain their personal goals. Again, I utilized an acronym to make the point. We concluded that all of our products were intended to solve five basic needs. The first letter of those needs became a potential acronym. We had a choice, use GIRLS or GRILS. We decided GRILS would be more appropriate. The needs are as follows.

Risk was a primary concern because of the possibility of dying too soon, living too long, or the hazards along the way. In asset management, we were concerned with the Growth, or appreciation, of the properties, the Income properties could generate, the Liquidity of those properties, and tax Shelter opportunities. We designed a chart based on those five considerations and the acronym of GRILS covered all the bases. Utilizing Growth, Risk, Income, Liquidity, and Shelter, we divided our planning into two areas of concern. One described as Risk Management and the other as Asset Management. All of this was illustrated in a simple chart, which is also included herein. By utilizing the wheel and the GRILS illustration, we were able to communicate in simple terms what our advisors would be doing and what products were available to organize an effective financial plan. Our organization was one of the early pioneers in this movement. Today, all the financial institutions have incorporated these products and services into their portfolios.

Figure 8.2

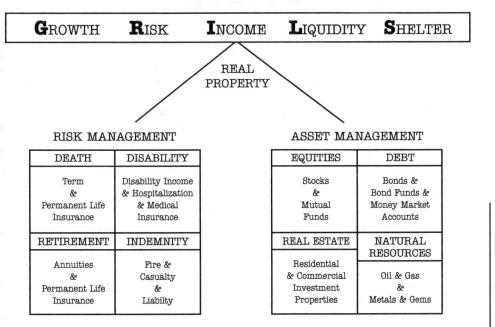

A DIVERSIFIED PORTFOLIO CUSTOMIZED TO ATTAIN YOUR PERSONAL GOALS AS THEY RELATE TO:

GROWTH   RISK   INCOME   LIQUIDITY   SHELTER

REAL PROPERTY

RISK MANAGEMENT

DEATH	DISABILITY
Term & Permanent Life Insurance	Disability Income & Hospitalization & Medical Insurance
RETIREMENT	INDEMNITY
Annuities & Permanent Life Insurance	Fire & Casualty & Liabilty

ASSET MANAGEMENT

EQUITIES	DEBT
Stocks & Mutual Funds	Bonds & Bond Funds & Money Market Accounts
REAL ESTATE	NATURAL RESOURCES
Residential & Commercial Investment Properties	Oil & Gas & Metals & Gems

What has happened to the financial service industry is called convergence. The one time specialty product institutions each began to diversify, and during the past few decades, banks, investment houses, property and casualty firms, and obviously life insurance firms began traveling similar routes and are now creating totally diversified portfolios and sales representatives that market accordingly. The personal story of the Levine Financial Group is well detailed in one of my earlier books entitled, *From Life Insurance To Diversification*, which was also published by The National Underwriter Company.

Convergence resulted in the margins of profit on many of the products that were now introduced to the financial advisors' portfolio being significantly different from product to product. At the same time, primarily because of inflation, the cost of doing business was constantly increasing. Convergence was the appropriate thing to do, but with lower profit margins and higher expenses, the principles of economy of scale and cost control became high priority items. Mergers and acquisitions led to big companies gobbling up the little ones in order to increase company size and create volume, to help offset the lower profit from individual sales.

Cost controls, as indicated earlier in this book, resulted in adjustments in the distribution systems, elimination of some training and recruiting activities, and an industry-wide trend of leaner and, sometimes meaner, administrations.

Nonetheless, companies, financial product salespeople, industry organizations, and regulators have all correctly decided financial advisors would better serve the consumer than "old style" product pushers.

Further, qualified and professional advisors would, in all their collective opinions, more effectively and profitably distribute all available products.

As I have already said, with convergence within the financial service industry now an established fact, most, if not all, of the financial service product manufacturers and distributors have portfolios that include all the diversified products their competitors also have available. These observations would seem to be good news for the consumer, the product manufacturer and distributor, the financial service companies, and most definitely, the agent, marketer, broker, advisor, or whomever is compensated by providing the products directly to the consumer.

Consistent with this trend, the National Association of Life Underwriters (NALU) changed its name to the National Association of Insurance and Financial Advisors (NAIFA). In Canada, the Canadian Association of Life Underwriters (CALU) changed its name to the Canadian Association of Insurance and Financial Advisors (CAIFA). MDRT has liberalized its qualification standards to include most financial products.

But what has really changed? Are the majority of distributors of financial service products really "advisors," or are they still pushing products like pharmacists push pills, rather than as physicians who first examine patients and then prescribe a solution for their patient's problems?

But what has really changed?

I am a speaker and trainer, whose clients include financial service companies, industry organizations, and aspiring "financial advisors," with a committed mission to help my clients become more effective and profitable by improving their "advising" and "people" skills. I admit to being shocked by the situation I find in almost all of my audiences.

I usually begin my presentations with at least three questions, which result in appropriate raising of hands.

Question 1: How many people do you see every week? I begin with 30 – to which very few, if any, hands are raised. 25, 20, 15, 10, 5? In almost every audience, over 50% have not raised their hands, even when I have gotten down to five.

Question 2: Do you always use a fact finder or standard questionnaire as a preface to your sales presentations? Less than 25% raise their hands. Remember, I am doing this to audiences of a great variety of clients, and they number in the cumulative thousands.

Question 3: Raise your hand if 80% or more of your compensation comes from a single primary product line, such as life insurance, LTC, health, D.I., annuities, investments, property and casualty, group pensions, etc. The great, great majority of every audience raise their hands.

My question to you, the reader, is how one can be an effective, productive, financial advisor if they are seeing less than five people per week, not using fact finders as part of the professional process, and primarily selling a specific product line that they are most comfortable selling in almost every situation.

Most companies have, at least on their shelves, all the materials and procedures necessary for achieving great success in the advisor process. The problem is their representatives don't use them.

Perhaps the financial service industry rushed to change their name and, hopefully, their image before they changed their actual professional practice. This is not an impossible mission. My experience has been that when the implementation of a solid financial advisor program is achieved, the representative enjoys greater income, greater self-satisfaction, and greater client respect and loyalty. The companies enjoy increased productivity and profitability, with greater use of all products in their portfolio. The regulator will see fewer complaints, and consumers will have better and more complete financial plans.

There appears to be a gap that must, and can, be bridged between the company and industry positions, which is to encourage total financial advising, and the field practitioner who, is "comfortable" only selling favored products to a friendly target market. Having been a long time practitioner, and having built a comprehensive full service financial service company, I know this bridge can be built. The key is starting the process by developing skills that will address the most difficult sale first, then developing a client relationship, and then address the total financial situation of the client.

I discovered this process from experience. Until the late 1960's, I was the General Agent/Manager of a successful life insurance agency. I decided, perhaps ahead of my time, to diversify and become a full service, all products, financial advisor agency.

It was an expensive challenge, but by 1975 we had a complete financial advising organization.

Those were exciting times and, if we were not the first to make that transition, we were certainly among the pioneers.

At first the productive results were extraordinary. We did tons of business and our former life agents, now "Financial Advisors," had income growth that was beyond their wildest dreams.

Then at the end of 1976 I discovered that I, and the Levine Financial Group (LFG), actually lost money that year. I couldn't believe it, and I began an analysis that took a full year to understand.

What was happening was my well-trained, successful, life agents were going back to their existing life clients and selling them all the new products in our portfolio.

It was easy because of the existing interpersonal relationships with their life clients and because of the marketing support they received from the LFG team. In many instances they enjoyed doubling, or tripling, their annual income while working significantly less. What a great deal, but I was losing money.

The analysis showed, though all other product sales were way up, life insurance sales were way down. The margins on all those new products were a fraction of the life insurance margins at a time when all our expenses, to provide the full financial services, had skyrocketed.

While all this was going on, I eventually discovered my previously well-disciplined life agents had stopped new prospecting, had compromised their basic sales skills, and had become product pushers.

Obviously, I tried to turn the ship around; but, once someone loses their discipline and sales skills, it is more difficult to relearn them than it was the first time around. Some of my previously better producers failed when they ran out of old clients to whom to sell the new products.

In time, we became profitable again because I learned how to manage a total financial service company and make it work effectively.

I believe prospects buy financial products for one of three reasons – greed, awareness of a need, or being sold, even though they were unaware of the problem or the solution.

> I believe prospects buy financial products for one of three reasons.

Greed is in all people to some degree. The prospect might ask, "What's in it for me – Profit? Appreciation? Tax advantages?" Investment people have capitalized on this human trait for years with smile and dial selling, which is rarely face-to-face, and though they might deny it, relatively easy.

Another type of prospect is aware of a need or want and is seeking a price reflective, good product. Examples are insurance for homeowners, automobile, health coverage, disability, group, cheap term, etc. A slightly more difficult sale, but one primarily based on product, price, and company comparisons.

The third group often begins the relationship with, "I don't need it, I don't want it, I can do better elsewhere." There is no urgent awareness of a need or want; there is suspicion, and sometimes a negative inter-relationship. This is typical of a life insurance sale situation and is by far the most difficult sale.

I have already mentioned the key is to begin with the "most difficult" sale.

To effectively face the unaware prospect, one must first sell oneself. There must be simpatico. Next, one must learn to listen, not talk, to uncover the dreams and aspirations of the prospect and only then, when this positioning has been accomplished, should an advising process begin.

While we have succeeded in my agency, the industry is still trying to get their sales teams to exploit convergence. The banks and investment firms have mostly failed in this effort. The P&C and health companies have done somewhat better, but actually also have fallen far short of their potential despite tremendous efforts.

Why? Greed and Aware sales, which are the foundation of banks and investment companies and property and casualty insurance firms, require a completely different sales skill, and it is very difficult to change the comfortable habits of a sales representative.

On the other hand, if one has achieved success in the unaware field, and has the skills leading to client relationships and achieved sales of the most difficult products, it is relatively simple, with proper training, to do total financial advising on a cross products all-inclusive basis.

That is how I solved my problem for the Levine Financial Group. Train all new advisors to develop the skill of the unaware sale, the life insurance and retirement sale, and discipline for constant prospecting activity. Once the unaware process is successfully completed, simply pick up the aware and greed sales, which are there for the asking. The actual advising procedures and techniques will be covered in total in Chapter 11.

These observations as to how we accommodated to change should be of value to every 21st century practitioner who intends to truly embrace the benefits of convergence. In my case, it took several decades of trial and error and expensive development to create what is today readily available from almost every company.

It has already been mentioned that one of the risks is losing the skills necessary to develop the activity one needs to replace the inevitable attrition of an existing clientele. I personally tried, and taught my associates as well, to always be certain to have five new starts every week, which guarantees that my clientele is constantly expanding. Further, I built an equalization formula, which I call the Unified Commission Credit, to determine how many dollars had to be put into each product line to end up with a comparable amount of compensation and expense allowance. This formula reflected the profit margins for me as a producer and as a manager, so that every dollar invested in any product was equated with a dollar in every other product.

Convergence has definitely changed the marketing of financial products, but it has also begun to level the playing field. At the moment, the life insurance specialist who is an expert in developing interpersonal relationships, making it possible to sell the unaware sale, has an advantage over all the other persuasions that have been product dependent rather than relationship dependent. With time and training that will change. In time every financial institution will have truly converged, not just in product and services, but in skills and techniques, and financial advisors will no longer be product prejudiced, but truly open minded consumer serving professionals. Many of the skills necessary to make this transition will be covered in some detail in subsequent chapters of this book. As I suggested when alluding to my coaching activities, the reader should reconfirm what they are doing, what they should be doing, and be objective enough to recognize what they are now doing, they should eliminate, and finally concentrate on the things they should be doing, making sure they continually keep doing them better.

Chapter 9

SEEING PEOPLE

In many ways the materials included in this chapter are the most important concepts in the entire book. The skills, techniques, and disciplines aggressively utilized in the 20th century that have either been lost or greatly eroded in the 21st century are those related to the financial advisor seeing many people. Another reason this is such an important subject is that the number one reason for many aspiring financial advisors to fail; they simply do not see, in fact they do not know how to see, enough people. An expression I heard many times in my early years was, if you didn't properly groom yourself every day, you would eventually become a bum. Also, if you chose to be a sales person of financial products, and you didn't prospect every day, you would also become a bum.

An acronym that I have used for many, many years is A-S-K. I have known from my earliest days in management that there are three attributes that every successful practitioner must have in order to be extraordinary. The National Association of Life Underwriters (now NAIFA) was so impressed with this concept that they did a video that was shown at local associations entitled, "Double or Nothing," utilizing this formula. A-S-K stands for Activity, Skill, and Knowledge. All three components interrelate. No matter how successful an individual is in one of the components, failing in one of the others will inevitably lead to failure. I illustrated this in the video, by suggesting if an individual graded him or herself on a scale of zero to three, with three being the maximum, and multiplied each by the other two components, you get a rating score. Using today's dollars, each point in the score would equal approximately $15,000 of first year commissions, though when I first used this formula $5,000 was the correct value. Therefore, if someone was adequate, but below average in all three categories and scored one in each of the components ((1 x 1) x 1 = 1), that individual would probably earn something in the range of $15,000 a year of first year commissions. The reason the video was entitled, "Double or Nothing" was because if they improved their capacity level in just one of the components, from one to two, and you did the same multiplication, you would end up with a total of two, or a potential of $30,000 of first year commissions. On the other hand, if someone was above average in each category and had a two in each

> An acronym that I have used for many, many years is A-S-K.

classification ((2 x 2) x 2 = 8), that individual has the potential of earning eight times $15,000, or $120,000 a year, plus renewals. The super producer, who already has more people to see than time to see them, gets a three for activity. If their skill level, particularly people skills, are also at a maximum level for another three, and they have designations, like CLU or CFP, and therefore, are also a three in knowledge, that totals 27 points, and they would be producing at the Top of the Table level of production.

Of course, this isn't an exact science, but it was remarkably accurate as a predictor for people I have coached and trained. In the real world, activity is the number one reason most people fail. It is possible that somebody would be below minimum in skills, or have absolutely no educational qualifications, and have zeroes in those categories but, I have never met practitioners who failed because of those categories. I have, however, known many practitioners who simply see too few people to survive in our industry. The reason can be found in the formula we just described. If under any category they scored a zero, zero times anything is still zero. Even if they excelled at skill and knowledge, with threes in both categories, but a zero in activity ((3 x 3) x 0 = 0), zero is still zero and the individual will most likely fail.

A good friend of mine, the late Fred Donaldson, from Enterprise, Alabama, used to tell a story that again makes the same point. He said that he had a friend who was a fantastic sales person and knew the business like a super expert. He was so skillful that he could sell to one out of every two people he ever met, but unfortunately, he failed. Whenever Freddy would tell that story, someone would ask, "If he was such a great salesman and could sell one out of two, how could he possibly fail?" With a big smile, Freddy would say, "He only had one problem, he didn't have enough twos." The point, of course, is that no matter how good his skill level, or how much the practitioner knows, you've got to see people to survive and excel as a product sales person or a financial advisor.

To use the "Double or Nothing" formula, the practitioner must be objective about the points scored in each category, or be graded by someone who understands the business and cares about the practitioner; that might be a manager in an agency. Once the weak suit is identified, concentrating on improving that point score will double one's income. In most cases, the weak suit will very likely be in the area of seeing people – activity. Many practitioners find skill development and knowledge much easier than facing call reluctance. Regardless of the point score, to really impact one's success in the business, an individual must focus on their weakest suit and be objective enough to identify it, and disciplined enough to work at improving it. This book is filled with skill ideas and concepts, and I have suggested the reader must get knowledge elsewhere. In this chapter, we will try to develop methods that, when properly applied, will contribute significantly to one improving their activity level and, thereby, improving the likelihood of achieving great success.

I will not attempt to educate the reader to the standard prospecting practices, since that information can be obtained from many other sources. I have found that the difference between an effective people person, who sees lots of people, and the individual who says, "I have no one to see" is not that they don't know the different prospecting techniques, but rather because they either have the psychological problem of call reluctance or they are unaware of what I have come to call the hidden curriculum. The techniques can be taught and the methodology is readily available to all practitioners, but the discipline and the capacity to implement those ideas are rarely, if ever, taught and monitored, and most people do not naturally have those talents. Someone has to teach them, or they will never master the skill.

Actually, we have already covered in the earlier chapters some of the necessary ingredients that may seem unrelated to prospecting and seeing people, but are essential to effectively conquer those people skills. We have discussed empowerment, and though we use the acronym B-E-A-K, the first two attributes necessary for empowerment are Belief and Enthusiasm. They are critical for every great prospector. The belief in yourself and what you do, and the great value it represents to a potential prospect, are essential to communicate, not only with the words, but also with the music, that the other person will be well-served to listen to your message. Further, the way you are perceived in terms of attitude and the excitement and enthusiasm that you communicate in your interpersonal relationships is contagious and powerful. When you combine belief and who you are and what you do with an enthusiastic and communicative personality, you have set the stage for effective prospecting. This is rarely, if ever, taught. The techniques of prospecting are frequently taught, but for many people it is not successfully implemented. Part of the reason relates to the empowerment and pecking order dominance of the communicative practitioner, as perceived by the potential prospect.

Also, as previously communicated, people are suspicious of all sales people, particularly in the financial persuasions, and communicating trustworthiness on the part of the practitioner compounds the likelihood of a successful ongoing interpersonal relationship. We have already used the acronym WINE CASK to identify the eight attributes I consider essential for building a 24 hour-a-day, seven day-a-week image that is perceived to be proof of the practitioner trustability. Attributes identified in that acronym that directly impact prospecting and seeing people are W for work ethic, which includes long hours during which the discipline of being a people person must be constantly implemented. Work ethic accountability, including the number of people seen, the number of prospects obtained, and the number of interviews conducted every working day must be one of the top priorities, if not the top priority for the effective practitioner.

People are suspicious of all sales people.

In the 20th century, the target for all new practitioners was to see at least 15 people a week in proper interviews. By the 1960's, two-interview selling became popular. Two-interview selling meant obtaining a fact finder on the first interview, and then going back on a second interview to present a solution for the prospect's problem, which meant that only five or six of those 15 interviews had to be starting interviews. The mission of that first visit was to sell yourself and obtain a fact finder. If a fact finder is obtained, a second interview is then necessary. Six new start interviews and four or five second interviews would assure more than 10 interviews per week. Besides those activities, some prospects required more than two interviews, some bought, which then required a delivery of policies-type interview, and in time as one's clientele built up, reviews for all clients required a certain number of interviews each week. Combining all those different activities would easily result in more than 15 interviews, which was the original target.

My good friend, Al Granum, is a legend in the financial service industry. After working with lots of new practitioners, he evolved the formula in his One Card System, which was universally embraced. It indicated if a representative contacted 10 people who were reasonably qualified and attempted to open a dialogue, three of them on average would evolve into new start type interviews. Typically, he found that those three interviews would again, on average, result in one sale. Therefore, to sustain the 15 interview outline I've just illustrated above, one would have to contact 20 people every week, from which they would hopefully obtain six bona fide interviews, which would, in time, result in two sales.

By now the reader should realize that in order to achieve the levels of activity that were the foundation of the financial service business in the 20th century, work ethic, and the discipline and accountability that goes with it, is still absolutely essential.

The second attribute under trustworthiness is Involvement. A recluse would have a difficult time in our business. Involvement is unto itself satisfying because the more things you do, that you enjoy doing, the better you feel about yourself. From a seeing people perspective, the more activities you have, the more people you meet. This not only contributes to the trusting relationships already discussed, but concurrently exposes you to a large number of people. This is essential for meeting your "seeing people" objectives.

The C – for compassion is another critical element in the hidden curriculum, which is rarely, if ever, taught. Potential prospects and referrers must believe that your primary motive is to help other people achieve their dreams and aspirations; not to self-serve by making sales and commissions. That attribute is closely related and intra-dependent with two other trusting attributes, attitude and skill. People do not want to meet with practitioners of any persuasion who are negative and communicate a losing attitude. Hence, being positive and acting like a winner are important pre-prospecting attributes that inter-relate with people skills. The charm and personality of the practitioner makes the potential prospect or referral feel comfortable in the interpersonal relationship. All of the empowerment and trusting skills are essential for the overall well-being and effectiveness of a practitioner, but several of them, which I have already indicated, are essential for getting to see lots of the right kind of people. This truth is rarely, if ever, taught as an essential for seeing people.

Some people are fortunate to have some of these attributes as a natural gift. For most people, it requires practice and time to build a persona that embraces all these attributes. If you are fortunate and already naturally enjoy some of these necessary attributes, you are well on your way, but begin practicing and refining those attributes that have not come naturally.

A good first step can be learned from the following experience I have had on many occasions when speaking to a variety of audiences of financial advisors worldwide. When I get to the subject of seeing people, I often ask the following question: How many of you see 30 people a week? Rarely do any hands go up. On occasion, one or two people will raise their hands. How about 25? Same reaction. Twenty? No difference. Fifteen? A few hands, but still very few. Ten? Not very many more. Five? It is quite normal for less than one half of the collective attendees to even raise their hands when I get to five.

The first great lesson from this exercise is that with the exception of the few, if any, hands that were raised when I asked how many saw 30, everyone else in the room had lied. If I asked that same question of a high school student or a librarian, or anyone not in commission selling, using exactly the same words, "How many of you see 30 people a week?" every person would raise their hands. The first mistake financial practitioners make is they separate people into potential sales and forget everyone else. I didn't ask how many people they saw to try to sell to them; I asked how many people did they see. I then ask if they can remember the time before they came into the financial service business, and they were just nice people. Nice people like nice people; there should be no difference in the interpersonal relationships of a financial advisor practitioner and the nice person who is not looking for a prospect.

The concepts of empowerment, trustworthiness, and being a nice person are the fundamentals upon which "seeing people" skills will be developed.

Let's discuss a few of the standard prospecting techniques and then the strategy that is the basis of my personal advising practice. It is also the key to the success of many of the people I have trained and coached.

As I have already suggested, most of the standard techniques and associated methodologies, except for the hidden curriculum additions we have already discussed, are readily available from every financial institution, in every book on the subject of selling financial products, and/or financial advising. Nonetheless, let me acknowledge that I have used all of the techniques I am about to mention, and I have taught them all to my associates; however, they have not been the primary methods of seeing people that I utilize and train my associates to implement. Since these methodologies are available through other sources, just for the record, let me mention some of the standards.

Direct mail is utilized by some practitioners effectively, but as a general rule, particularly today when it is aggressively pursued by almost every marketing organization, it is rarely the solution for an individual to see enough people.

Telephone solicitation, another of the standard techniques, has lost some of its effectiveness because a tremendous number of potential prospects in the United

States have exercised their right to restrict the use of their telephones for solicitation calls. Though at one time telephone solicitation did generate significant activity, it has become a far more limited restricted source.

Cold canvas, which is in effect what I was doing when I was selling Fuller Brush, can work if intensively pursued with tremendous discipline and long hours. Most of the people I know who have used cold canvas as a significant source of prospects, eventually burned out and either failed or evolved into some other kind of prospecting methodology, which they found less onerous.

Referred leads are the fourth of the standard procedures, and a primary prospecting source and methodology is very valuable. Once again, however, the hidden curriculum problem causes problems. Practitioners are taught to make a practice of requesting referred leads, and they are often told how to do it. Many, however, lose interest in that method after a short experiment because, for many practitioners, the results are disappointing. What is not effectively taught is that referred leads, which can be very valuable, are not any name one gets from any person. Random names forced from a prospect or client, or friend, is often little better than the names in the phone book. One must understand that the power referred lead presumes certain characteristics that are rarely taught and understood.

The solicitor of referred leads must understand that no power referred lead will ever be recommended if the referrer is not sincerely trying to help somebody. That somebody can be the practitioner and might be the practitioner's father, brother, or best friend who might, without any concern for the potential negative reaction of the referral, give names to the practitioner because they sincerely want to help the financial advisor. There are very few of those kinds of people in a practitioner's life and they are known as "centers of influence." Another potential center of influence can be developed if the practitioner has done a tremendous favor for the individual, or there is a bonded interrelationship and helping for the success of the practitioner is the primary motive on the part of the referrer. Centers of influence will give names that are power referred leads.

> No power referred lead will ever be recommended if the referrer is not sincerely trying to help somebody.

The second type of power referral can be obtained from people who sincerely want to help improve the situation of the referral. To obtain that kind of referral, the referrer must believe that the work and service the practitioner provides will greatly improve the well-being of the person to whom the practitioner is referred. Without the motivation of truly wanting to help some person, it is very difficult to obtain power referrals.

How do you define a power referral as opposed to any other name? If the practitioner aggressively pursues referred leads, until the potential referrer is prepared to give names just to get rid of the practitioner, they will get names of people who are of no great significance to the referrer. They don't want to be embarrassed by someone who really matters to them, and/or gets annoyed that they gave their name to a sales person. Many practitioners aggressively pursue names from people they meet – prospects, clients, friends, and acquaintances – and then discover that either they cannot get an interview with the referral, or if they do get an interview, it is generally unsuccessful. Chances are they got the names of people who are not significant in the lives of the referrer. Power referred leads presume that the referrer is respected and has great influence over the referee. It could be a relative, a very close friend, or business associate. Those relationships are protected and would only be shared for the two reasons already explained above – to help the practitioner or to help the referral. If the results from seeking referrals do not prove profitable, most practitioners stop asking for names.

Another consideration is the referral must be a qualified prospect for the advisor's target market. Target markets differ from practitioner to practitioner, but they generally can be measured by the financial situation of the potential prospect, the marital status, the occupation, the age, and the potential prospect's physical well-being. Communicating your expectations to the potential referrer, after a strong inter-personal relationship is established, is very important for two reasons. First, it helps the referrer know what type of person you are looking for, and second, it improves the probability of a client relationship being developed.

Direct mail, cold canvas, telephone solicitation, and referred leads are all techniques that the practitioner should be aware exist, but of those four, only referred leads are a must for every practitioner. Direct mail, telephone solicitation, and cold canvas are specialty areas that only a select few practitioners should actually pursue.

Another more current technique has recently evolved, and that is seminar selling. This is also not for everyone. However, there are many in the financial service industry who get most of their prospects by running seminars on a regular basis. They direct their presentations to some specialty area of expertise.

My experience has been that to dabble in seminar selling is generally a waste of time. The great majority of the effective seminar providers sustain it over a long period of time. Along the way, they have developed a complete package of procedures for pre-meeting marketing, administrative systems, usually involving staff, a powerful and impressive presentation, including power points, a target market that fits their specialty, and often offer an inducement, such as a free lunch or dinner at a desirable location. It usually takes a sustained effort to build a reputation and a following where the audiences justify the cost and the effort.

It is not my intention to recommend and promote any of the techniques already discussed over any other. However, in the past, as well as among today's cutting edge practitioners, referred leads, social mobility, and the inter-personal skills of the practitioner already discussed are the common denominators of successful practitioners. It is those three methodologies that were the key to my personal practice, both as the source of prospects, who ultimately became clients, and as the source of potential recruits to join my organization. Those three sources require a high skill level for the practitioner.

Interestingly, I have no problem speaking from the platform to thousands of people, but I have never been a very effective sociable person in day-to-day living situations. I love people, but I'm not good at small talk. Fortunately, my wife, Sandy, is outstanding in those areas. She remembers people and their names, can easily strike up a conversation with strangers, and can mix wonderfully at social functions. Those are a natural gift, which I envy but clearly lack. On the other hand, I figured out early in my career that overcoming that weakness was essential if I was going to excel as a financial advisor. I, therefore, had to create a technique, which I have since discovered is transferable and very effective. I call this approach "the non-interview."

I call this approach "the non-interview."

The Million Dollar Round Table learned of my technique 20 years ago and asked me to speak on the main platform, describing this methodology for the audience. I have had the privilege of being on the main platform at the Million Dollar Round Table on eight different occasions and have done an untold number of afternoon workshops. This was the only time they specifically asked me to speak on a specific subject. I spoke in Dallas at the annual meeting and had an extraordinary audience reaction. What surprised me the most, however, was that several of my good friends, whose names I included among the heroes in an earlier chapter, individually, and out of the ear shot of the others, told me they loved the talk, but what I described was essentially what they themselves did in developing their prospects. I heard that many times from industry greats. What I thought I had discovered and that was uniquely mine, was a method being utilized by other industry super stars. However, it had never been spoken about, never was given a name, nor was it ever included in any of the training materials within our industry. It was a unique method used by successful people who had figured it out themselves, as a way of achieving the mission of seeing lots of people.

To learn how to be an effective non-interviewer, let's suppose you were in a non-threatening occupation, so once again presume you are a librarian. You are invited to a dinner party, and all of the attendees are people you have never met before. You visit over pre-dinner cocktails and then sit with people on either side of you at the dinner table. At the start of the evening they were all strangers. Before dinner was over, it is highly likely you, the librarian, with no personal motive or self-serving interest, would know the name of several people at the dinner, would know their occupation, their marital status, whether or not they had children, and you might have a pretty good guesstimate as to their level of affluence. This would be normal for a nice person talking to a nice person, but incidentally, it is also an important part of a financial advisors fact finder. Earlier in this chapter we established that everybody sees significantly more than 30 people a week, and if we could once again be nice people, we could talk to more than 30 people a week. I didn't say sell to them or try to have a formal interview: I simply said we could, from a social perspective, talk to them. You could do that in line at the supermarket, in your office building, in the neighborhood in which you reside, at organizational meetings, or just about any place. A nice person without the inhibition of thinking interview and commission would certainly learn, as did the librarian, the name, occupation, marital status, etc., about this nice person you just recently met. Of course, many people might be unreceptive and cold in their inter-personal relationships and, therefore, not become an ongoing acquaintance. However, using Granum's 10-3-1 formula that is just fine since we only need six new starts a week. But the great majority would enjoy someone else taking the initiative in the right place, at the right time to start a conversation.

To test if you have lost your interpersonal nice person skills, let me ask you a question: "Do you know the name of your physician's spouse and whether or not he or she has children? Do you know the names of the children?" I ask these questions of large audiences, and the great, great majority do not have a clue. This is the same physician that will tell the patient to take off all their clothes, stand naked before them, and ask the most embarrassing questions, while touching the most private parts of one's anatomy. Even though that relationship has gone on for years, the patient has never taken the time and trouble to ask the physician, are you married – do you have children, etc. Physician aside, do you really talk to everyone you meet, every day?

Financial advising is a people business and, along with empowerment and trustworthiness, one must develop inter-personal relationship skills in order to meet nice people, not necessarily to ever sell to them. As I said, I myself am not a natural small talker, so I had to figure out when I meet these nice people, wherever that might be, what do I say and what do I do. I discovered that for me asking questions was easier than talking. This is most appropriate because the skills required to be an effective advisor instead of being a product-pushing sales person, include the capacity to ask questions and then listen to the answer. You don't just listen with your ears, you listen with your eyes and your heart, and you must learn to feel the other person if you are really going to excel at questions and listening. So when I meet somebody, whether it is a waiter in a restaurant or my doctor, or someone at an organizational meeting or a dinner party, rather than clumsily trying to force a conversation, I introduce myself by name and then ask for theirs.

The reason I call this procedure the non-interview is because it cannot be scripted; it must be the nice person's personality and charm and great flexibility conversing with the new contact. However, I do direct the questioning into four specific areas. The most common being the family situation – are they married, do they have children, where do they live, where do they work. If I don't get a positive and enthusiastic reply to any of the above, I might then pursue their business relationships – do they own their own business, did they build it themselves, etc. Sometimes neither of those will get much of a reaction, particularly among single people, and then I might ask questions relating to self-serving issues – retirement, homes, cars, lifestyle, etc. Finally, for some people if none of the above seems appropriate, I might pursue questions relating to community, arts, charities, etc. These are not one-way questions. In order to have a comfortable dialogue, I find it very easy to respond in kind to their answers to my questions. They can talk about their family, and I'll talk about mine. They can talk about their work, and I will talk about mine. There is never a piece of paper visible, or any indication this is anything other than a friendly visit between two nice people talking.

I can tell if they are simpatico by the way the questions are answered. If the answers to the questions I ask are shorter than the question, I am not doing real well. Are you married? – Yep. Do you have kids? – Two. It isn't going famously. However, are you married? – Yes I am. I'm married to my childhood sweetheart, and she's a partner in my life and my business. We have a couple of great kids, and they are on sport teams at school, etc., etc. – then I'm doing good. They wouldn't answer like that if they weren't comfortable with me. And comfort is what I'm looking for.

I'm often asked, "Well how often do you do non-interviews?" I try to speak to at least 30 people a week without any business motivation built into that activity. It is not unusual for me to do non-interviews with the same individual many times, over a long period of time, perhaps a year or more. I don't proceed beyond the non-interview until I feel I have established a comfortable relationship. On the other hand, I have on occasion started a conversation with someone, where within minutes, we were totally comfortable with each other and I might immediately transition to a real business interview. If I do enough non-interviews every week, the cumulative effect is that I eventually will have a tremendous pool filled with lots and lots of people. Some will become just acquaintances or budding friends, but some eventually might have the potential of a business relationship. One of the attributes of empowerment is to have more people to see (under the A for activity) than you have time to see. Non-interviews over a long period of time guarantee the inevitability of achieving that level of activity.

Non-interview relationships, however, are initially not business-based, and at some point, though the practitioner has established a relationship of sorts, you must learn when it is appropriate to attempt to transition from social to business. There are four questions that I suggest you ask yourself to help determine when it is time to attempt to transition.

First, have we established a level of simpatico – mutual respect and trust? Is this someone I would like to be with and I think they would like to be with me?

Second, is this person in my target market area, someone I would even want to pursue? Over the years I have moved my target expectations up significantly. When I first began, I would talk to anybody who could see lightning and could hear thunder. But slowly I became more selective until I established certain requirements before I would spend time with any individual prospect. Knowing your target market, and only pursuing people who fit your expectations, saves a great deal of time and energy and is very effective.

Third, is it time to transition and if so, when and where? The great majority of non-interviews either become acquaintances, perhaps friends, or disappear from my life and never get into the transitional stage because they don't fit my expectations.

I'm doing the rejecting, rather than the prospect. If I do decide that I want to see the person, I want to do it under favorable circumstances, so I will pick the place. If I have done a good job of selling myself and building an interpersonal relationship with the potential prospect, and they trust me and I have a pecking order equality or dominance, I can pretty well tell them when I'd like to see them and rarely, if ever, do they say no. Of course, I suggest that what I have to show them will be of great value to them, and it is certainly worth a few minutes of our time to find out if what I would like to discuss would be beneficial in helping them achieve their goals and their aspirations.

The fourth question I ask myself relates to their hot button. I've asked them a lot of questions, and I've gotten to know what's important to them. Usually, somewhere along the line, I have detected a hot button that is a high priority in their life, and clearly, it is one of their more ambitious goals. This helps determine which of the many different financial advising procedures and product lines are most likely to be of the greatest interest to them.

So in summary, if I have done an affective job during the non-interview process, I have built a strong simpatico. I know they are in my target market, I have capitalized on our inter-relationship to specify a time and place we ought to get together, perhaps for a cup of coffee, or in their home, or more likely in my own office. Finally, I have prepared in my own mind the direction of the interview when we do get together.

Remember, this can be after one non-interview, or 10 over a long period of time. But that big pool is filled with lots of wonderful people I've gotten to know and who have gotten to know me, from which I only need five or six new starts a week to more than achieve my 15 interviews a week target.

A non-interview is not in any textbook. It is like many of the things we have alluded to in this book that I call the hidden curriculum and can only be learned and comfortably implemented with practice, practice, practice. It is the preface for every potential advising situation, even when a formal business interview has already been scheduled. For example, if I get a strong referred lead, and the referral knows that I will be speaking to them about financial advising, since I've already done some work for a close friend or associate, and they've agreed to visit with me, I am nonetheless meeting them for the very first time. Therefore, before I begin a financial advising interview, I would begin with a non-interview. I might begin by saying something like this: "Mr. Prospect, we have never met, but our mutual friend tells me you are a wonderful human being who I really ought to get to know. If you don't mind, before we talk business, I'd like to spend a few minutes to get to know you better. For example, he never even told me if you were married or had kids. Would you mind sharing with me your family situation?" Then shut up and listen. Let the potential prospect talk. Try to establish a strong inter-personal relationship. It might take 10 minutes; it might take an hour; but do not move towards a business interview until you have sold yourself, or built something of a trusting and comfortable inter-relationship. If you run out of time on

A non-interview is not in any textbook.

that interview because of the pleasantries of getting to know each other better, no harm done. Simply reschedule a formal interview, and the next time it will be a great deal easier to proceed with the intimacies of a true fact-finding financial advising first interview.

Another fact about our wonderful business is it gets easier and better as the practitioner becomes more effective in building a clientele. All financial advisors must stay in touch with all of their clients on a regular basis. Situations change. With our variety of products, the appropriateness of any individual product is constantly in a state of flux. Clients need updated advice on a regular basis. The larger the client, the more complex the situation, the more frequent the reviews. For example, when a practitioner develops a clientele of at least 300 clients, not customers, but clients, and there is an inter-personal relationship and programs in place, annual reviews become a significant source of activity. If that practitioner works a 50 week year, annual reviews, presuming you only meet a client once a year – although the bigger clients you would see more often – would generate at least six interviews a week just to update the existing programs. I separated my clients based on the size and complexity, their future potential, and the simpatico relationship, into A, B, and C clients. The A's were the largest, with the greatest potential and the strongest inter-personal relationships. The B's, one notch less, and the C's less again. The C's I classically delegated to people in my organization. I saw all the A type clients a minimum of three times a year, once being totally social, utilizing theater tickets or whatever as the basis of the get together, and the other two to update their program. Interviews were set automatically by my staff, and this was a very efficient way of maintaining my clientele. I saw the B's once or twice a year for business, and on occasion socially. I would only occasionally visit the C's, but most of them were delegated away. Nonetheless, once I matured my practice to where I had a significant client base, my problem wasn't seeing 15 people a week; it was finding the time to see them.

My annual review procedure is worth sharing, and I know many of my associates and coaching students have embraced the procedure. My wife, Sandy, is a completely dedicated professional in her own right. She has been part of my business world, along with my social world and is an invaluable partner. When I met her she had been widowed for over a year because her husband had passed away of a heart attack when he was only 40 years of age. She was left with an 8-year old son and limited financial resources. Though her husband, by coincidence, was also in the life insurance business, he had only a small amount of life insurance. She had not been prepared to be a widow and, therefore, was unaware of most of their financial positions. Fortunately, the manager of the agency that her husband had represented with New York Life voluntarily came to her assistance and between them they were able to settle the relatively small estate. When our relationship became serious and we decided to marry, she proposed the following: Each year we have what she called a contingency day. We would spend the entire day together and make a listing of all of our assets and specify where each was located and how to get access to them. We would review any legal work, such as Wills and Trusts, and make sure they were up to date. She wanted to know everything, as a reaction for all the things she didn't know after her first husband had passed away. As I write this, we have been married for 38 years. At least once every year, we meet for breakfast, spend the entire day making a written record of our total holdings, and then finish with dinner.

Initially, I created a property book in which we recorded all this information. It had tabs in the book for bank accounts, investments, life insurance, property and casualty insurance, health and disability insurance, attorney's name and address and Wills and Trusts, accountant's name and address, burial arrangements, including cemetery, plots purchased, etc. Dutifully, each year the book was updated and, in recent years, this information has been transferred to the computer.

I was so impressed with the concept, I mass produced the property books and gave them to each of my clients. I added a page in the front where we schedule on an annual basis, or more often for the "A" clients, our next review visit. When we initiate the property book, I tell Sandy's story and suggest, at least for the married clients, that they consider having an annual contingency day for their family. Though additional product sales were never the motivation for the creation of the property book, almost every time I do a review with an existing client, and we turn the tabs in the book to see if there have been any changes since our last visit, inevitably the question of inadequate or missing coverage becomes part of the conversation and usually results in additional sales.

The real message, however, is that doing reviews is essential to an ongoing financial advising relationship. As we reach the end of this most important subject, seeing people, I think it is important that we expand the implications of seeing people beyond just the financial advisor practitioner. I have often been asked how it was possible for me to be a significant personal producer at well above the million dollar round table level, and occasionally at the top of the table level, and at the same time build a major financial advising organization, while concurrently being an industry activist, writing books, and speaking all over the world. The answer is that there may be multiple job descriptions in my biography, but they all share one common skill – seeing people. When I do 30 non-interviews a week, and I'm involved in many organizations exposing me to large numbers of people, I am concurrently finding new friends, some of whom are power brokers I can use in the future. Using the non-interview technique, I found potential prospects for me as a producer and potential candidates for recruits in my agency. I was opening doors for each of the different challenges in my life. As the manager of a financial service organization, the greatest challenge, and therefore the highest priority, was recruiting new associates. So before I ever considered if a new acquaintance was a potential prospect as a client, I evaluated if they were a prospect for a career change.

In Chapter 11, I will be sharing the procedure I use for implementing a financial program, but it is the same procedure I use for selling a career. Therefore, when you combine the skills for seeing people with the skills for implementing a program, you are actually a cutting edge practitioner for building an organization, establishing a new clientele, and finding volunteers for a cause to which you have dedicated some of your volunteer time. Great financial advisors, super organizational managers, and extraordinary volunteers in organizations are all sales people who have excelled in developing their own people skills and using those skills on large numbers of people.

Chapter 10

CONCEPTS AND MISSION

Thus far I have shared some timeless skills, techniques, and concepts that are the foundation for a successful financial advisor. In the next chapter, I will share the procedure I use and teach for implementing effective advising. However, before we get to the actual advising process, it is appropriate to share some fundamental ideas and concepts to reinforce our effectiveness and to be certain that our career mission is achieved. The stories I am about to share serve a double purpose. First, they should contribute to the mindset of the practitioner to help affirm that passion and compassion are one's primary career motivation. Second, these stories can be told to prospective clients to help them recognize the absolute necessity of a good solid financial plan.

One of the most important fundamentals of a successful financial advisor is understanding and communicating what is known as "human life value." There is no way to replace the emotional loss of a loved one, or of a business executive. However, every human being represents an economic value without which their families and business associates would suffer the double loss of emotion and economic hardships. In every financial plan replacing that potential economic loss, which I've already expressed as "dying too soon," is obviously a high priority. Even though most prospects, and the practitioners in our advising industry, understand the concept of human life value, as a general rule, they grossly underestimate its true meaning.

> One of the most important fundamentals of a successful financial advisor is understanding and communicating "human life value."

As an illustration, none of us will ever forget the tragedy of 9/11 and the World Trade Center Towers destroyed by terrorists. Approximately 3,000 people lost their lives that day. Most of their families and businesses have subsequently faced devastating economic difficulties. Insurance programs, the government, and charitable benefactors pooled resources to provide some compensation for the families of those who died that day. The combined benefit from the three sources averaged approximately $3 million per deceased. That benefit was greatly influenced by each deceased individual's human life value. Consideration was given to the age of the deceased, his or her level of compensation, their family situation, and their business replacement value. In effect, those who decided how much each individual family should receive applied the basic principles that every financial advisor should use in making recommendations for a financial plan. I don't intend to do an editorial on how I feel about government contributing to those payouts, but with good financial advising, each individual should have had a self-created program to offset the potential economic loss. In contrast, since the beginning of our great nation, servicemen have died to preserve our freedom and have never received more than a tiny fraction of the World Trade Center payouts. They have been encouraged to buy personal life insurance to protect against that sort of tragedy. Of course, 9/11 was an extraordinary event and resulted in extraordinary reactions.

We practitioners have a challenge, because if our clients' families don't receive benefits from the Federal government, as the result of litigation after an accident, or from community contributions, the people we try to help will be totally dependent on their own financial plan. In other words, if someone died of a heart attack or cancer, the only thing they would leave behind is that which they themselves created.

Let us consider whether $3 million was an appropriate payout. For many of our prospects that is too little. So why do most people think it is too much? That sum of money might need to last a lifetime for the beneficiaries. In order to be certain that the beneficiaries don't outlive their money and end up losing their dignity when they become dependent on government or family, it is desirable that the basic principle, in this case $3 million, is not invaded. They should live on the income from that money. Three million dollars in a safe investment would generate about $150,000 a year, which would be taxable. That would leave approximately $100,000 a year that could be spent for living expenses. That's a respectable sum, but not out of line for families with college educations and home mortgages as part of their current lifestyle. If a breadwinner making $150,000 a year died at the age of 45, the individual would have earned over $3 million plus benefits over the next 20 year period, prior to retirement and without pay increases. Said another way, the individual was, in effect, a money making machine that had an economic value of over $3 million.

So far, these calculations would seem to indicate that $3 million is not an inadequate amount. However, it is likely to be too little. Most of us know and use the rule of 72. It is usually used to illustrate how quickly money will double if invested at a predictable rate of interest. If you divide the annual rate of interest, say 5%, into 72, in approximately 14 years that money would double in value. If you invested $1,000 at 5%, in 14 years it would be worth $2,000. Using the same rule of 72 applied to the cost-of-living, because of inflation, the cost-of-living also inches up. If inflation was at the rate of 3½% or more annually, the current cost of living will double in approximately 20 years. Therefore, if someone needs $150,000 in today's money, that potential beneficiary will need $300,000 for the same lifestyle by the 20th year.

So far, we have only addressed dying too soon. Using the same concept, what happens if you live too long? Wealth accumulation must be a top priority during the earning years. It must provide a retirement with dignity when one has to, or chooses to, stop working. If $3 million was the appropriate amount of principle required per beneficiary to comfortably sustain $100,000 a year of after tax income, that same number must be accumulated for retirement. Most people think their social security and corporate pension benefits are enough to sustain a comfortable retirement. As I mentioned in the early part of this book, most corporate and government plans are under funded. They may or may not be available at full value at retirement. Certainly, they are a wonderful benefit that should not be ignored, but they should not be a total plan for concerned individuals. Besides, Social Security income is also taxed if the individual is reasonably, economically comfortable. Most corporate plans presume the continued existence of the sponsor company but even if the company does survive, it doesn't guarantee it will not have to restructure the pension plan. If the combined benefit of Social Security and the corporate plan held up and were projected to be $6,000 a month, it would only provide $72,000 per year. Besides that number being suspect, the cost-of-living will inevitably be significantly greater and in 20 years the $150,000 per month retirement requirement will be $300,000, and that $3 million of necessary principle will be $6 million.

When I built my financial plan, I presumed I would need a predetermined income from my wealth accumulation years, which on paper seemed more than adequate. When I reached 65, my calculations were verified, and there was more than enough money to live with dignity. Now almost 20 years later, I have personally experienced what I've just shared, and it turned out to be exactly correct. My cost of living has doubled because of inflation and lifestyle, and hopefully I still have many more years ahead. If I had grossly under funded, I would be forced to make severe cutbacks in my lifestyle and could conceivably be facing the loss of independence and dignity.

Unfortunately, there are additional, sometimes ignored, considerations. My grandparents died in their 60's, my parents in their 70's, and today life expectancies are moving up to the 80's, 90's, and 100's. It was relatively easy to create a retirement plan for someone who would only live a few years beyond retirement. With the current life expectancy continuing to increase, 30 years of retirement is not only reasonable, it may be an understatement. If you consider human life value, project it with the cost of inflation, reduce the probability of some government and corporate plans, and then extend life expectancy, it should be obvious to every practitioner that we must raise our sights in financial planning. It is our mission to provide adequate income for all three hazards of life. To implement these plans, it is often necessary to share these human life concepts with our prospects and clients. Of course, all the amounts mentioned above are just to make a point, and must be adjusted for each individual's capacity and aspirations.

Unfortunately, there are additional, sometimes ignored, considerations.

The practitioner must think "big" to effectively communicate what it takes to assure a comfortable living based on the prospects' dreams and expectations.

One final thought on human life value. Most of your prospects own a home and an automobile. They are valuable, but not nearly as valuable, even from a purely economic perspective, as one's life and the lives of the people they love.

In all probability, their home and auto are fully insured for full replacement value. You might point out that even if their home or auto were destroyed and there was no insurance, but they were alive, well, and working, they would find a way to replace those properties.

Does it make good sense to fully insure properties worth a lot less than their very being, while woefully under insuring their most valuable asset, their capacity to produce an income?

If they were killed in an accident, their families would sue the driver, airline, or whomever, for $10 million or more; but they self-insure for a lot less than their real economic value.

Another basic for the professional financial advisor to consider is that if they are doing only part of the job, it might turn out to doing none of the job. As I have stated several times in this book, there are three broad areas of risk – dying too soon, living too long, and the hazards that can occur along the way. Most product pushers do a good job addressing one of the three problems. A good financial advisor addresses all three. It is impossible to predict which of these risks is likely to create a catastrophic situation for a client. In applying Murphy's Law, much too often when a risk becomes a reality, it is in an area that was not properly protected. Most clients who believe they have a top professional advisor will be loyal to that advisor and not consult competitors. Therefore, the advisor becomes an excuse for not doing what other professionals might recommend. Of course, every prospect or client will not implement every part of the recommended program. However, it behooves the professional advisor to at least introduce and, then, encourage action for each of the three broad risk areas.

My experience in coaching and training has reinforced this belief. Most experienced advisors have significant client files, which are filled with tremendous vacuums. Many advisors are sitting on a big pond of prospects who are existing clients that have not addressed all three risk areas. As I suggested in the chapter on convergence, many of my associates did a tremendous job, with their existing clientele, of filling the vacuums that existed because they previously did not have a full financial portfolio. We solved that problem in our organization, but it still exists for many practitioners even though they all now have complete portfolios.

When I recruited a new advisor for our organization, I guaranteed them that if they followed my instructions they would be millionaires within 10 years. Wealth accumulation is just as important for the practitioner as it is for their clientele. As a matter of fact, by exercising appropriate procedures for their own wealth accumulation, the practitioner will feel more comfortable recommending it to their future clients. The premise of my millionaire commitment was on several very simple practices.

First, by utilizing all of our financial products, I tried to get my associates to a level of first year commissions exceeding $100,000. In fact, our agency averaged per capita first year commissions well in excess of $100,000. I then suggested they take 10% of their first year commissions and invest it or save it. In each subsequent year, they should live entirely on 90% of their first year commissions, again saving 10%, plus all their renewals. Their investments should include appreciating property like their home, or equity products, along with some guaranteed products. The plan was that simple, 10% of all first year commissions with 100% of all renewals and concurrently investing in properties that appreciate. As promised, all of my associates who had produced $100,000 or more first year commissions and bought appropriate investments were millionaires, usually in less than 10 years. The interesting point is that most of them came into the business in debt, with no real assets.

I'm speaking about practitioners or prospects earning over $100,000 a year and I know that at the turn of the century that was well above average. But let's establish two important principles. First, when the income levels are less, say $60,000 a year, perhaps from combined income of a client and spouse, the principles we have established are still the same. The numbers are smaller, but all of the rules of human life value, the rule of 72, and wealth accumulation are the same, only proportionately less. Second, most people tend to think small and their dreams are not big enough. One of the intangible benefits of having a good financial advisor is the practitioner can help raise the sights, dreams, and expectations of the people they are advising.

Risk tolerance is obviously a significant factor in making recommendations of investment products. The practitioner's own perception of what the problem is, and how much risk the client should take, is not a key issue in an advising process. The advisor must be open minded and listen, as we've already stated, not just with the ears, but with the eyes and the heart. The advisor must develop the skill of being sensitive to the true feelings of a potential prospect. Too often, advisors push their clients to make financial commitments beyond their capacity. Even worse, they may imply high rates of return, often accompanied by high risk, for people who are either not in a position to take such risks, or not inclined to do so. Financial advisors should lean toward the conservative side, and adjust to the desires of the prospect/client.

> Risk tolerance is obviously a significant factor in making recommendations of investment type products.

The great John Savage had a sales presentation that he shared from the platform many times. When he had completed a recommendation for insurance and savings, and the client agreed to a substantial annual financial commitment, he then often said, "We can do that next year. Let's cut your commitment down to a level that we know will be comfortable this year." He also would suggest there are three basic places to put money – the bank, investments, and insurance. He would get the now reduced financial commitment and divide it between the three different instruments, in appropriate allocations. At the end of the year, he would review the financial results. Usually the only one of the three investment opportunities that had been totally maintained was the insurance commitment because it required a fixed deposit and, psychologically, wasn't liquid. The amounts contributed to investments and the bank were usually way under funded. Sometimes adequate money had been deposited in those other investment vehicles, but it was then withdrawn for emergencies or some item they wanted to purchase. There are a lot of lessons to learn from this Savage overview. The practitioner should never over sell, should recognize that discipline and accountability does not come easily and must be taught, and the client will have a chance to reevaluate and reestablish a financial plan at the annual review. Also, if there isn't some discipline and accountability, they may under deposit or withdraw, thus failing to complete the plan.

If our prospects and clients have time, they can adjust a financial plan and build wealth accumulation over a period of years. If they are unfortunate and die too soon, the only practical immediate solution is life insurance. When a prospect cannot implement an entire plan during the initial advising interviews, at the very least the greatest short-term hazard, dying too soon, could and should be addressed. The rest of the plan can be implemented over a period of time, but not necessarily immediately.

Everything we have discussed from Chapter 4 to this chapter has been intended to utilize the hidden curriculum, while getting the practitioner's mind set to be all powerful in the actual process of financial advising. In the next chapter, we will describe the advising procedure, but first I would like to illustrate by sharing an actual case that almost ended in failure. However, because of the techniques we have already discussed, the case was salvaged and became one of the biggest cases I ever implemented.

Some years ago, a very good friend gave me a wonderful referred lead to one of the largest ranchers/farmers in the entire country. He told me that they had about 100,000 acres under cultivation and because most of their assets were tied up in relatively non-liquid land, they had a very serious potential estate tax problem. With his help, I was able to get a confirmed interview. The problem was the ranch was a four hour drive from my home and they wanted to see me at nine o'clock in the morning. I had a commitment the night before so I couldn't leave and stay over night near the prospects, so I had to leave the house for the appointment shortly after 4:00 a.m. I'm a pretty good morning person, but I need a full night's sleep and obviously I wasn't going to get one.

Nonetheless, I was on the road at 4:00 a.m., very tired and very irritable. I got to the prospects' town in time for a cup of coffee, which helped a little, and I arrived at the prospects' ranch well before 9:00 a.m. Thanks to our mutual friend. I knew a lot about the prospects, and I also knew their problem, which had been confirmed by their accountant. The meeting began with the two brothers who owned and ran the ranch, their accountant, and their attorney. I, tired and irritable, didn't do my usual non-interview. I immediately took out my fact finder and began to ask very personal questions. I asked about the size of their estate, their previous planning, their family situation, their taxes, etc. The older brother reacted very quickly with: "Who do you think you are, a San Francisco city slicker coming down to see us country bumpkins with a carpetbag in your hand?" Wow, had I blown it? It was like a cold splash of water in my face because I knew he was right. I had not done a non-interview, I had not even tried to sell myself. I did not shut-up and listen. I knew what the problem was, and had not done my usual non-interview, but how do you fix it?

My response, fortunately, worked and went something like this: "Mr. Prospect, I'm sorry and you are right. What you've just seen is not me. I got up at three o'clock this morning and had very little sleep because I was working last night. I drove four hours to get here, and I was irritable and cranky, and I admit it. You've seen me at my worst. I apologize. With your permission, I would like to take a few minutes more, but not to try to sell you anything. I promise I will not ask any personal questions. I would just like to leave with you having a better impression of me and me getting to know you better. Our mutual friend knows what kind of person I am, and he will attest that what you've just seen is an embarrassment and one I would like to correct.

Well, the brothers had compassion and said, "What would you suggest we do?" I said, "Well, I'd like to get to know you better. Would you tell me about yourself and about the ranch?" I shut-up and listened. They told me how their father had started the ranch and how they had expanded it to a tremendous size. It now had its own cotton gin, tens of thousands of acres of cotton under irrigation, its own crop dusting airport with four crop dusters and two passenger planes, one a jet and one prop driven. They grew tomatoes and had a tomato canning plant, and each had their own homes on the ranch. That gave me a chance to also talk about my background, and they were impressed with my agricultural major in college and, as it also turned out, we were politically of the same inclination. After well over an hour, there was obviously a developing simpatico. As we approached lunch hour, I thought I'd be leaving for home, but they said, "Why don't you stay and have lunch with us?" They took me to one of their homes, we had a fantastic meal prepared by their house staff, and then they asked if I would like to see the ranch. I said, "I'd love it." We got into one of their vehicles and toured the ranch. I saw their private airport, the cotton gin, the fields of produce, and the tomato canning plant; it was like a storybook afternoon. As the afternoon shadows lengthened, it was obvious I had to start my four hour trip back home. We never had gotten close to talking about financial advising or any products.

As I was about to leave, I made the following suggestion. I said I was going to have some mutual friends contact them and tell them what I'm really like. I'm going to send you some materials about me and my organization. I believe I can be of help. I'm sorry we got off to a bad start, but with your permission, after a couple of weeks I'll call, and if you want to see me again, I'd be delighted to come down and perhaps help with your problems. Then, I got in my car and drove home.

I did all of the above; they received phone calls from mutual friends and received my materials in the mail. After two weeks, I picked up the phone and called again. The older brother, who had called me a carpetbagger, answered the phone and when he heard my voice started laughing. He said, "Norman do me a favor and call off the dogs. I've gotten nothing but phone calls and mail, and I'm convinced you are probably all right and we'd love to see you again. This time, so you don't show up cranky and irritable, we'll send the jet to San Francisco and fly you down, so you can get here refreshed. We'll see if perhaps you can help us with our problems."

As they suggested, I flew down for the second trip, for the first time, did a proper fact finder, and took a look at what they already had done in financial planning. They showed me trust instruments, which had been funded by insurance ostensibly to offset estate taxes. However, when I read the agreement, I realized who ever drafted it was unfamiliar with a proper trust intended to help with estate taxes, and had in effect put the insurance proceeds back into their estate. I told them my opinion and they were shocked, particularly because the attorney who drafted the agreement was a son-in-law. Incidentally, I subsequently had a high powered tax attorney in San Francisco look at that trust and confirm my impression. But on that interview, I told them they were woefully under insured, and regardless of the old trust, I recommended creating a new and proper one and funding it adequately to cover the potential tax liability. There were four lives involved, the two brothers and their wives, and the initial sale which was consummated on that second visit was for premiums in excess of $700,000 a year, which eventually grew to well over $1 million a year. Unfortunately, the older brother, whom by then I called friend, had a serious physical condition that resulted in a highly rated policy. Fortunately, they took the policy because, within a year, that brother got out of his jet plane at an airport and, while walking to the terminal, dropped dead of a severe heart attack, and we had our first claim.

Our advice about the first trust proved to be correct because the Internal Revenue Service disallowed the tax protection of the previous trust so those proceeds were included in their estate. But my policies and the trust agreement fully passed the IRS investigation. Several additional sales over the years were consummated on the remaining three principles and some key persons among their employees. Eventually, the two spouses also died, and the death claims obviously were very large. The surviving brother has significantly cut back on the size of the operation and is enjoying a healthy retirement.

Without people skills to salvage an apparently lost cause, and then without a full day of non-interviewing, none of this would ever have happened. Empowerment, and the ability to develop a trusting relationship under pressure, led to a client relationship that otherwise would never have been developed. Millions of dollars of estate property would never have been saved for the survivors, the taxes would never have been offset, and the surviving brother would have been in serious financial stress.

> Without people skills to salvage an apparently lost cause none of this would ever have happened.

I share this story to position us for the next chapter. These concepts, along with empowerment B-E-A-K, trustworthiness W I N E C A S K, and the non-interview are all essential techniques and concepts as a preface to client inter-relationships. They are rarely taught, but make a tremendous difference. They are the fiber of the whole person, whether in a non-interview, a social or family situation, or in a business interview. They are timeless techniques that should be embraced by every 21st century financial advisor, and they will contribute to a very successful professional practice.

Chapter 11

FINANCIAL ADVISING PROCEDURES

All of the chapters in Part Two are intended to position the reader to implement financial plans as practitioners for effective financial advising. It has been said that everyone can sell someone, but no one can sell every one. That means one's effectiveness as an advisor is not very different than the batting average of a ball player. The advisor can improve their effectiveness and, thereby, their income and ability to assist the consumer, by either implementing more plans or increasing the size of the plans. Or better yet, by doing both concurrently. The techniques I have already described as the hidden curriculum are the methodologies for significantly improving one's advising batting average. It began with empowerment, which is a combination of belief, enthusiasm, activity, and knowledge. It is strongly reinforced by trusting relationships with potential clients, which can be measured by work ethic, involvement, no broken promises, ethics and morality, compassion, attitude, skills, particularly people skills, and knowledge. The activity level can be greatly reinforced by utilizing the non-interview concept at least 30 times a week. Human life values and the introduction of the impact of inflation would result in more appropriate and, most likely, larger solutions to one's individual financial problems. When all of these techniques and concepts are integrated into the very being of the financial advisor, the practitioner approaches a client properly positioned to begin a business interrelationship. As already stated, everyone can sell someone, but the batting average is often geometrically improved when the mindset and image of the practitioner has been maximized by utilizing the positioning techniques mentioned above.

Earlier in this book I mentioned Al Granum's One Card System and, most particularly, his 10-3-1 formula. Contact 10 people, get three solid interviews, and close one sale. For the purest life insurance sales person that formula is absolutely correct. However, in the diversified financial product advisor world, I have found that 10-5-3 is perhaps more accurate. The reason is that every single person we ever approach is likely to buy one of the products in our portfolio from somebody every single year. Depending on how diversified the practitioner's portfolio, they annually renew their homeowners and automobile policies; they are likely to contribute to a savings or retirement plan, probably using an investment type vehicle; they may or may not need hospitalization or some form of health, disability, or long-term care coverage; and they will, in fact, using the 10-3-1 formula, be a potential candidate for life insurance. If the average qualified prospect is likely to buy at least one of the products in an advisor's portfolio, it becomes obvious that the successful advisor ought to sell something at better than a 10-3-1 ratio. With the practitioner's ability to sell him- or herself, pecking order dominance, and the people skills already discussed, the ability to sell is greatly enhanced for the diversified advisor.

Since selling oneself is an important attribute for effective financial advising, let me share a story that I experienced that reinforces how effective selling oneself can be. I was on a speaking tour through Asia. I began in Singapore and noticed that I wasn't feeling sharp. I moved on to Kuala Lumpur in Malaysia, by which time I was feeling pretty terrible. I had red bumps on the right side of my face and my right eye was beginning to close. I knew I wasn't feeling well, but initially didn't even share it with my wife.

> Selling oneself is an important attribute for effective financial advising.

While in Kuala Lumpur, she noticed the red bumps and my eye beginning to close and asked me what was going on. I admitted I didn't know, but I wasn't feeling very well. I had to speak several times in Malaysia and then in Thailand before returning home. A commitment is a commitment, so I had no intention of aborting my trip and hoped the problems would go away.

My host in Malaysia, when advised of the problem, said we had to go to a doctor, which I rejected. I was not comfortable going to a doctor in a foreign country, speaking to someone who didn't speak English, and with facilities that were not up to U. S. standards. My host insisted I go and said he would act as translator. Reluctantly, I finally agreed, but had absolutely no intention of following the instructions of this as yet unknown physician. My host took me to a local clinic, which again reinforced my reluctance, since it was not new and modern, nor was it very clean.

I was introduced to a Chinese doctor, whose primary language was Chinese, but he also spoke Malay, and my host spoke both languages. The physician had invited me and my wife, along with the translator, into a very comfortable office and suggested we sit down. He said he would like to ask me a few questions. To my surprise, the questions had nothing to do with the medical situation. He asked where I came from, what my family situation was, what I did for a living and, through the translator, we were into a very interesting, "non-interview." I began to like the doctor even though he couldn't speak my language, and I became more and more comfortable with each passing minute.

We must have visited on a social level for at least a half hour before he finally said, "Well tell me what is bothering you?" I described the symptoms and the way I felt, and he suggested I join him in his treatment room for an exam. He was quite gentle and very efficient in checking out my symptoms. We then returned to his more comfortable office and again he asked me to be seated. Through the translator he said, "I had nothing to worry about." What I had was shingles, a disease I had heard of but never really understood, and with simple treatment it should be completely gone by the time I got home. He gave me medication for my eyes, and a pill to take and said that there was no question I'd be fine in a matter of days.

When I went to meet him, I had absolutely no intention of following his orders or taking whatever medications he prescribed. But afterward, I liked and trusted him enough to follow his instructions. I did precisely what he suggested, and as he said, within days the condition completely cleared up and my eyes were fine. I thought I had invented the non-interview, and here was a perfect example of its effective use. This Malaysian doctor had earned my trust and confidence, and convinced me of his medical expertise, which led to the appropriate medications and a complete recovery. When I returned home, my own physician confirmed everything I had been told.

Supposing, however, the doctor had been in a comparable unkempt facility, and the moment we met he rushed me into an examination, and said I was fortunate because that day they had a special on pink pills. I could get a gross of the pills at a 50% discount, and if I took the pills I would get completely better. No non-interview, no trusting relationship, just a product pusher, anxious to get to the next patient. There is no way I would have taken those pills, and chances are my condition would have worsened. Professional practitioners, be they physicians or advisors, greatly improve their effectiveness by selling themselves and their expertise before attempting to prescribe a medication or product. So utilizing all the techniques we have already discussed as a preface to any sales or advisor situation is time and energy well spent.

Before I describe the procedure that I have found to be very effective, there are some ground rules worth mentioning. It is not my intention to provide the reader with a specific sales track and presentation. There are lots of sales tracks available, which can be memorized and utilized. They all work, if done properly. Whichever sales track the advisor is comfortable utilizing is compatible with the following procedure. Another important point is that though most advisor procedures require two or perhaps three interviews, there is no absolute requirement for any particular number of interviews. I have sometimes done non-interviews multiple times with the same person, over a period of a year or more, before transitioning to a business relationship. On other occasions, I have made sales in one business interview. So the number of non-interviews and business interviews is totally flexible and dependent on the time being right to proceed.

Another important rule is that during the positioning part of the procedure I am about to describe, the advisor should never be confrontational, adversarial, or mention a product or cost. The prospect is always right, at least during the positioning part of the relationship. If there was a confrontation or adversarial issue, even if the practitioner won the fight, there is a good chance he would have lost the war. If tension exists between the prospect and the advisor, it is likely they would not be able to implement the program at the conclusion

The advisor should never be confrontational, adversarial, or mention a product or cost.

of their visit. Any question about product or price should be deferred until the entire procedure is completed. This can be done, quite simply, by the advisor suggesting he or she does not know if there would be any product involved, or what it would cost, until we have precisely established what are the dreams and aspirations of the prospect. At that point, the advisor will be able to recommend a plan to help the prospect achieve their dream.

The procedure has an acronym to remind the practitioner of the sequence that must be followed. The acronym is the word "action" – A-C-T-I-O-N. The first five letters, A, C, T, I, and O are steps that I call the positioning portion of the procedure and must be completed sequentially before proceeding to "N". The final step, N, which stands for "now you make a sale or implement a plan," is never attempted until positioning is complete. With the rules of the procedure firmly in place, we can proceed with the process.

A Aspirations. That is another way of saying their dreams, their expectations, and most particularly their wants. During the non-interview, the practitioner should have developed an interrelationship with simpatico and should have been successful in uncovering the prospects' dreams and aspirations. Without that being accomplished, an advising procedure should be delayed until those objectives have been completed. Only when the prospects' answers to the advisor's questions are longer than the question, and the prospects voluntarily share what is important to them, should a transition to a business interview be attempted. Since "aspiration" is the first step in the advising procedure, I utilize the non-interview technique to ask questions in four different areas – family, business, self-serving, and philanthropic and community. When I get proper answers to my questions, I have a pretty good idea of what is important to the prospects and what they really want. As I've already suggested, this might happen in five minutes, or it might take five or 10 different non-interviews, spread over a long period of time. I do not attempt to transition from the social non-interview relationship to a more formal business relationship until I am comfortable that both simpatico and the wants of the prospect have been established. Once achieved, I will capitalize on the comfort level that exists to transition to a business relationship. It can either be started immediately, or scheduled for some time in the future. Rarely, if I have read the prospects' feelings toward me correctly, do I ever get turned down for a serious business interview. Sometimes I have to offer myself as a second opinion because they may feel that they have already addressed their financial planning. With simpatico there is no resistance to having a cup of coffee or a brief visit to determine if I can be of valuable service in helping them achieve their dreams and aspirations. Once the transition from social to business has been accomplished, the "A" of action has been successfully accomplished.

Using this procedure it is important to never go from one letter in the acronym to the next until successfully finishing the previous letter.

C Current Situation. Since I believe in want selling, not need selling, I have never thought of a fact finder as a way of uncovering need. I use the fact finder or data information sheet for determining what the prospects' current situation is, as it relates to achieving their dreams and aspirations. You can use any sales track with a fact finder to get that information, but my target is to find out what they have already done about achieving what they really want. The fact finder provides the details as to their personal and family situation, as well as their assets and liabilities. The great majority of prospects are under funded for even remotely attaining their aspirations when facing the three universal risk areas – living too long, dying too soon, and the hazards along the way. Of course, on occasion, someone who already has a plan is adequately funded. Even in those cases, however, it is not unusual to find a lack of the necessary legal documentation to implement their plan – Wills, Trusts, Agreements, etc. On other occasions, certain necessary areas of protection have been totally neglected, even though most of the plan has been implemented. If the prospect has a fully funded, adequately documented, and complete financial plan, they may not be a prospect but rather a great source for other referrals.

A much more likely situation is the prospects have no plan whatsoever, or they have one that is inadequate to achieve their objectives. In any case, with A and C completed, it is often self-evident, even without eventually doing all the technical calculations that the prospects are in an extremely vulnerable position. That brings us to letter "T".

T   Taking Away the Prospects' Dream. On some occasions, the practitioner can move from "C" to "T" in the same interview, but for many advisors it is appropriate to take the information they have acquired, leave, do a complete analysis, and return at a future date for the next interview. The financial advisor knows that the current plan, or lack of one, precludes the prospects' dreams ever being a reality. The next step is to make certain the prospects understand that, as they are currently positioned, their dream cannot happen if any of the three life's risks become a reality. This must be done with compassion, not a club. In the old days, a salesman product pusher might back up the hearse and scream, "You are going to die or you are going to live too long." The modern advisor must show compassion and concern for the present plan's shortcoming. You can communicate the shortfall by making sure it is obvious you really care. It might be expressed with words something like this: "Mr. Prospect, I know what you really want, and I'm here to help you get it. I also now know what you have done in your current planning to achieve those aspirations. It is obvious, with the way you are currently positioned, you will not be able to obtain your dreams and goals with your present plan. Perhaps there is some asset or future assets that you didn't share with me when we filled out the data sheet. For example, is it possible that you will be inheriting some money that we've never talked about, or that you have some company benefit plans that you forgot to include?" And once again use the listen, don't talk technique and shut up. In all likelihood their response will eventually be something like this: "Norman I've never thought about it, but it is obvious that my family and I are at risk if something unfortunate should occur. However, I have not left anything out, and I have mentioned all of the assets that I now have, and I don't anticipate any windfalls in the future."

By taking away their dream with compassion rather than with a baseball bat, the prospect is obviously thinking and perhaps for the first time facing the reality that what they want is not what they have. At that point we have sequentially completed A, C and T, which brings us to "I".

I Implied Concern. "I" is critical and cannot be overlooked. Many salesmen have been taught to use the closing technique of implied consent, and that is not an inappropriate technique; but this "implied" serves another purpose. Before we try to implement the plan and sell products, it is important that the prospects acknowledge that they have a problem. Don't forget the Malaysian doctor. They will not buy pink pills, or any product, unless they are convinced it will help them solve their problems. The reason for the "I" for implied concern is that many people find it difficult to verbalize their concerns, but when you listen with your ears, your eyes, and your heart, it is obvious when the prospects are concerned. Often it is non-verbal, but implied. In any instance, verbal or non-verbal, if the prospects do not show a concern for their shortfall, you should not continue the procedure, but should go back to review the previous steps. You should not proceed to the next step until their real concern is obvious. Restate their dreams and aspirations and review what they have done about them. Do they agree that what they've done about it will not achieve the desired results, and once again, are they concerned. If they are not concerned, you do not have a prospect. Continue to try and get some acknowledgement of a problem, or terminate the interview. Without the acknowledgment of a problem, they will not purchase a plan. However, once "I" is done effectively, the advisor is ready to move on to "O".

O Offer them Back their Dream. You might say something like this: "Mr. Prospect, I know what it is that you want, and I admire you for your good judgment. We also know that with the way you are currently positioned, what you want is not likely to happen. On the other hand, I commend you for your concern, which makes it all the more special for me personally to be here. That is because I am in a position to show you a way to make all your dreams come true. What you aspire to is obtainable. Let me ask you this. If I could show you a way to achieve the security and well being to which you aspire, in a way that you can comfortably afford, am I correct that you would be interested in seeing such a plan?" When you get an affirmative answer to that question you would have completed the positioning part of the procedure. Let me remind you that you can use any sales presentation for the words, but what we are talking about here is the music. You must sequentially complete each step of the action process before proceeding to the next step. That might take one interview or five interviews, but it is going to materially improve your batting average, so don't skip steps, or move too quickly. With positioning complete, we get to the last letter "N".

O - Offer them Back their Dream.

N "Now" You Can Implement the Plan or Sell Products. All of the standard closing techniques can be effectively utilized, but in most cases, if you have properly positioned yourself, the plan implementation is almost certain. All that might be required is some negotiation. The prospects may not be in a position to implement the entire plan immediately, but should recognize, with some sense of urgency, the need to at least initiate a plan. That might be accomplished by not addressing all the risks immediately, or not fully funding human life value at this time. It might mean temporary solutions like term insurance, supplemented by some savings. No two situations are the same. I earlier suggested the 10-3-1 Granum formula is correct for just life insurance. The 10-5-3 formula may be too conservative when the diversified portfolio that all practitioners currently enjoy is fully utilized.

It has been my personal experience, and the experience of my most successful associates, that if they do fully position the prospect with A-C-T-I-O before attempting to implement a plan or sell products, their closing ratio should be very close to one for one, presuming they don't start the count until they get to "N" – Now they close.

This advisor concept using the procedure of A-C-T-I-O-N is as appropriate for anyone selling anything. In financial services, managers often seek new advisors for their organization. If they do lots of non-interviews every week, some candidates will be identified. For example, when managers attempt to recruit, they would be well served to then use the exact same acronym in their recruiting process. To be most effective in recruiting, first determine the dreams and aspirations of the possible candidate. If those dreams and aspirations are consistent with the minimal expectations of the manager the process can continue.

The next challenge: Is the current situation of that candidate going to help them achieve their dreams and aspirations? If yes, it may be difficult to get them to change career direction; but if not, they very likely will want to listen to a better opportunity. That brings us to the manager taking away the candidate's dreams and aspirations in their current position and encouraging them to consider an advisor career, where their expectations can be achieved. If the prospect shows concern and frustration from the realization that their career is a dead end street, we have completed "I" – Implied Concern.

Continue the procedure by implementing the "O" part of the acronym. Share all the great attributes of the successful financial advising career. Presuming the interrelationship has been effectively positioned, the next step would begin to actually go through the selection procedure leading to a career - A-C-T-I-O-N. For recruiting is exactly the same as A-C-T-I-O-N for advising, or just about any other sales situation. In both instances, be it for a recruit or prospect, the mission is to help the candidate or the prospect achieve their dream, which incidentally will help the advisor or manager achieve their own objectives. Win-win is the only way to go, and this procedure assures that everybody wins.

Chapter 12

MENTORING AND SUCCESSORSHIP

For the struggling new practitioner, the subject of this chapter may seem to be less exciting and, perhaps, less urgent than the subjects we have already covered. In the long run, that's most certainly not the case; but even in the short run, some of the material we are about to address will have practical applications for all practitioners. For the matured, successful practitioner, the subjects are critical for their career's future well being, and the survivorship of the fantastic industry we all represent.

Let me begin by going back to some material we have already discussed. Some of the major differences between the last century and modern times is there is substantially less recruiting, training, and education for the developing practitioner. Many companies seem to have lost their direction and their original mission, and many managers who are responsible for recruiting and training are frightfully distracted by compliance, administration, cost control, and survivorship.

Many companies seem to have lost their direction and their original mission.

Even if they had the time, it is likely that many managers don't even know what many practitioners call the religion of our business. They probably also don't know what we have been describing in this book as the hidden curriculum, which are the non-text book, timeless techniques that make the best practitioners successful. If you do not have the time, skill, or knowledge to succeed as an advisor, and then the capacity to effectively pass it on to the next generation, a serious void in advisor development exists. That void must be filled by some other means, and this chapter will address an excellent alternative.

I learned the religion of our business, in part from my mentors and manager, and in part because, unlike many of my peers, quite a few of my early sales resulted in early claims. For example, shortly after my Fuller Brush experience, I was doing aggressive telephone and direct mail solicitation. One direct mail reply led to a fairly difficult interview with someone who lived not too far from my home. He was a contractor with a wife and three children, and their home was fairly impressive in a nice neighborhood, but the backyard was filled with construction equipment and the inside of the house was rather disheveled. I did a classic programming sales presentation, which then required a great deal of aggressive closing, but finally resulted in a sale. The wife was very helpful. It was a policy known as the Family Income Policy, and though it only had $10,000 of permanent insurance with a decreasing term rider, it created a potential death benefit of almost $50,000, in those days a fairly substantial sum of money. They agreed to pay the premium on a quarterly basis, and I collected the first premium. The policy was issued standard, and I delivered the policy. The wife told me she was very grateful for my effort.

When the second quarterly premium came due, I received a late notice from the company indicating the premium had not been paid. The client wasn't far from my home, and I stopped by and again had to do a complete sales presentation to collect the second premium. The same thing happened with the third quarterly premium, but happily the policy was kept in force. Shortly after collecting the third quarterly premium, I left for my first company qualifying convention at a fancy New England hotel. While at the meeting, my phone rang and the wife was on the phone to let me know that she was now a widow. The husband, who had been a heavy smoker, became quite ill and, at first, his physician thought it was pneumonia. When they got him into the hospital and did a complete exam, they discovered it was lung cancer; they operated unsuccessfully and he died in the hospital. That was my first death claim. When the check was issued, since the widow had requested a lump sum settlement rather than an extended payout, I went to the home to deliver the nearly $50,000 check. At that point, I was in my mid-20s and the widow, at least by my perception, was an older woman, though she was probably only about 35. She opened the door, and when she saw me, immediately started crying, threw her arms around me, and hugged me so tight I couldn't get away. I still remember that strange feeling, partly from elation in having been in a position to bring some hope to their home, partially in discomfort at being hugged by this crying older woman.

When she regained her composure, we went into the home, and I completed the delivery of the check. She then shared a story I knew nothing about until that moment. They did have three children, two of them natural born, but one was in the adoption process, which was not yet completed. When the breadwinner died, the State threatened to take the third child away from her. She went to court and argued to keep the child. She explained that her parents owned a farm in upstate New York, and she would move to their home. This meant there would be very little financial responsibility, and the parents would be there to assist in raising the children. Unto itself that didn't appear to be enough to satisfy the judge, but then she remembered the life insurance. She explained her husband had almost $50,000 of life insurance on his life, which she would be receiving. Between the new home and the significant amount of cash, there was no question she could properly raise all three children in a very comfortable lifestyle. The judge ruled the adoption was permanent and final.

The tears she shed when I rang the doorbell were a reflection of her happiness and gratitude for the life insurance policy that had almost not been sold, and on two occasions had almost lapsed. It's been well over 50 years since I rang that doorbell, and I still feel the emotion that the miracle of life insurance brought forth on that day.

There were other claims, one for disability for a permanently disabled good friend of the family, and another for life insurance where a new father drowned in a boating accident, all within the first year of my post-Fuller Brush life insurance career.

My wife, Sandy, thanks to a modest but adequate financial program that her first husband had provided, was able to live with dignity, though she did take a job after being widowed. She, however, was able to avoid the desperate widow dating world, and through mutual friends, we found each other and have been happily married for almost 40 years. I doubt that we would have ever met had it not been for her economic ability to stay in her own world after the tragic loss of her husband.

Love and compassion are the foundation on which dedicated financial advisors build their practice. This kind of "religion" was discussed at every life underwriter meeting, and every agency and company meeting, in the 20th century. It is rarely, if ever, discussed today.

> Love and compassion are the basis for a dedicated financial advisor to build his or her practice.

As I said earlier in this book, the practicality of continuing education at meetings often overrides the communication of emotion and skill development, which I consider essential for great financial advisors. The question, therefore, is how does the modern day practitioner get that motivation and inspiration if the company and the manager are distracted, and the industry organizations no longer emphasize the impact of the miracle we carry in our attaché case?

There is an organization called the Life Insurance Foundation (LIFE), which receives contributions from individuals and companies to be used for public relations and advertising efforts to communicate the miracle of proper financial advising. They do an extraordinary job sharing stories, not unlike my early death claim mentioned above, and constantly reinforce our true mission. They have materials that are used in classrooms and are available to practitioners to give to, or share with, their prospects and clients. I strongly recommend utilizing that fantastic resource for communicating the religion of the business.

One of the expressions they frequently feature is "Life Insurance is for the Living." That is really what it is all about. It isn't the sale, the volume, or the commission; it is for the people who need help the most. And then a proper financial program is there at the right time with the right solution.

If we can't count on management and companies to do an effective job with most of the new practitioners coming into the business, and for those already practicing who are struggling, what alternative exists? Happily, there is an answer. A few years ago, the Million Dollar Round Table (MDRT) contacted me and asked if I would become chairman of a special committee, which would be known as the Mentoring Task Force. They warned me that others who had attempted to create such a program faced industry objections and had failed in the attempt to implement such a plan. There were some mentoring programs in some companies and agencies, but they were rigid, required mandatory split commissions, and involved a specific job description.

Though they worked in selected situations, most agencies and practitioners refused to accept those conditions. Another issue was that many producers resented managers and companies trying to exploit their expertise to do the job that managers were getting paid to do in the first place. Some managers and management organizations also rejected the concept because they felt the MDRT might have been usurping their responsibility by trying to find an alternate method of distribution for the skills and best practices required in the financial service industry.

They asked me to take over the chairmanship of the committee because I was a past national president of the General Agents and Managers Association (GAMA), a past national president of the Life Underwriters Association, a past vice president of the MDRT. They thought I might be a potential catalyst for bringing all the different groups together. With the rocky beginning behind us, we realized that the key to any mentoring program that would get the approval of all the different groups was flexibility. Within months, we created a program that could be utilized any way a mentor and aspirant wanted to use it. The pairings were to be an MDRT mentor who would be working with someone who aspired to become a member of the Million Dollar Round Table. The relationship could be whatever seemed appropriate, based on the inclinations of the mentor and the aspirant. In some instances, the relationship was little more than a cup of coffee once a week with motivation and inspiration and accountability built into the visit. While in other cases, it involved daily training, supervision, joint work, and anything in between.

A system was set up to establish a customized relationship between the mentor and aspirant, and part of the agreement was determining what each had to do in their ongoing relationship. These decisions could include education, joint work, split commissions, personality differentials, activity levels, etc. All were negotiated and agreed to before the relationship actually became effective.

We went to the different organizations within the industry, explained the program, and were able to get the unqualified endorsement and support of all the groups who had previously been resistant. The MDRT members who represented the bulk of the mentors considered it a contribution to the well being of the industry, not an attempt to get them to do the job of the company and the manager.

With the complete endorsement of the different institutions within the industry, it was decided to begin with a pilot group of 40 mentor/aspirant pairs within months of the time the committee was first initiated. The results of the pilot group were extraordinary. Eighty percent of the aspirants qualified to attend the Million Dollar Round Table in the first year. Equally exciting was the fact that the mentors averaged a 20% increase in productivity during that same period. The bottom line – the mentor, the aspirant, the companies, and the industry all profited from the mentoring concept.

Mentoring is still an ongoing program, now jointly sponsored by GAMA and MDRT, and a council has been created with an equal number of board members from each organization, with a rotating chairmanship. That is the council that maintains and supervises the industry mentoring program. MDRT administers the program from its offices in Illinois, and the program has already had thousands of mentoring/aspirant pairs with ongoing results comparable to the original pilot group. The Round Table has allowed aspirants, meeting 80% of the necessary qualifications, to attend an MDRT meeting with their mentor to introduce them to the MDRT experience. A great majority of the aspirants, however, fully qualify and attend as qualifying members.

Getting back to the religion of the business, it is obvious that the skills, hidden curriculum, and religion of the business exist primarily in the established, successful financial advisor. The successful advisor is the most available and valuable resource for communicating the miracle and the religion of the financial service business. No individual is better positioned to pass the baton from one generation to the next than the successful practitioner.

One caution for those who might be considering getting into a mentoring relationship is that it is easier and less stressful to reach agreements on all issues, most definitely including commission compensation, before there is money on the table. Part of the mentoring process includes establishing, in advance, if and when there would be commission splits, what the percentages will be, who will get the renewals, and who will be responsible for servicing the client. Once established, it doesn't matter whether tens of thousands of dollars of commissions become part of the relationship, or just a few dollars or nothing at all. There cannot be an argument about the arrangement after the fact, if it is properly established before the fact.

Another important factor is that the aspirant is required to send a report to the mentoring council once a month, preferably signed by the aspirant, the mentor, and the manager (if there is one), which builds serious accountability into the program. We learned early on in this process that without accountability, the program was significantly less effective.

> Without accountability the program was significantly less effective.

A significant by-product of the mentoring process relates to another major issue for a financial advising practitioner. Early in my career one of my heroes, who for privacy reasons will remain nameless, was one of the superstars of The Aetna, the first company I represented. I admired him greatly and picked his brain at every opportunity. With no warning, one day I learned he had been to the doctor the day before and had been diagnosed with terminal cancer. He never really came back to the office, but I would visit him at his home and during his final days in the hospital. He shared with me a great concern. He had spent a lifetime building a tremendous practice and his clients were his mission and his true love. He was an expert and had treated them professionally, with their well being his primary motive. He knew that when he passed away there was no arrangement for successorship, and he was greatly concerned that his clients would be poorly served, and the programs he had established over his lifetime would quickly crumble. In my naiveté I assured him that it wouldn't happen, but I was very wrong.

Soon after he died, many senior agents in our organization, most of whom were not nearly as professionally qualified as my deceased friend, went to the manager and demanded the names and client files of the deceased for their own personal use. The manager was weak and fearful of losing the affection of these aggressive profit centers, and within a month of my friend's departure all of his client files were distributed to other agents in our office. I, and the other new people, didn't get any, which was fine, but I couldn't believe what I saw happen. Wherever possible these marginally unethical agents, who in effect had robbed the grave of a super hero, went about attempting to replace, and thereby earn new commissions, the business my friend and mentor had properly written during his lifetime. The clients, in my opinion, were abused, the company's reputation was tarnished, and the professional image of our good practitioners certainly suffered.

After I reached a reasonable level of success, the MDRT came to me and asked me to chair a committee to be known as The Professional Practice Continuation Committee. We met for over two years, and the results of our investigation were eventually printed in a book by the MDRT entitled, "Professional Practice Continuation." It pointed out that without a successorship plan, what had happened to my friend could happen to you. It showed that companies frequently presume the policy holder or client belongs to them, not the financial advising practitioner. As a matter of fact, several of my friends and I have been expert witnesses in trials where a practitioner got into a disagreement with a company about who was entitled to service and maintain the relationship with existing clients. Sometimes the agents won and sometimes the companies won. The point is a pre-arrangement is desirable.

Some companies allow current practitioners to make arrangements with a potential successor and, in those cases, there is no problem if the practitioner finds and makes an agreement with a proper protégé.

When a company does not allow that kind of relationship, one of the vehicles that many practitioners utilize is the corporate entity. Again, that presumes the existence of corporate contracts with the companies they represent, but a corporation survives the death of a principle and continuity is assured. At the very least, having a successor, even without a legal document, comfortable with the existing clientele is most desirable. If the client knows the successor and is inclined to work with him or her in the absence of the original practitioner, with or without agreements, there is a likelihood of some continuity. The client really decides who they will work with.

One of the best ways to find that successor would be to use the mentoring program. Either a brand new recruit trained and developed by the mentor can grow into a successorship position, or an existing agent who is struggling might be embraced as an aspirant and developed as a successor.

One of the best ways to find that successor would be to use the mentoring program.

There is another reason to consider such a plan. Of course, the obvious one is the well-being of the client and the reputation of our industry; but future income, including renewals, normally flows to the heirs of the deceased practitioner. If some unethical practitioners replace the existing business, not only does it adversely affect the client, but it also has a direct negative impact on the income of the heirs.

Before I close this chapter a related issue, which is rarely addressed, concerns what some of us in the industry have called "menopause." Obviously, it is not the physical menopause, but rather an emotional change in a practitioner's enthusiasm and effectiveness.

A case in point, but not atypical, was when a good friend of mine, who I had always considered a very successful financial advisor, approached me at a meeting and said, "Norman, I don't know what to do, I'm simply burned out. I'm bored, I don't like going to the office in the morning, I have no enthusiasm for what I'm doing, and frankly, I'm even thinking of getting out of the business. Have you any suggestions?" Those symptoms are clear evidence of the existence of what I, and some others, call "career menopause."

I asked him to join me for a lunch the next day, and I was prepared to make many suggestions. We had a delightful visit, and then I addressed the issue of what he might consider doing. I suggested he consider making a completely new start. He was financially comfortable and what I suggested was easily within his means. I said you might want to get a brand new office, redecorate and furnish it, hire an additional assistant, develop a new logo, letterhead, etc. I further suggested he should consider working with a protégé/aspirant and divide his clients into those he truly enjoyed being with and who also have the greatest potential for challenging, additional financial requirements in the future. I also suggested that he stop working with people he didn't enjoy, or people who did not have a challenging and interesting situation. To be certain those people are properly serviced, his new aspirant should be assigned all of those clients and prospects.

I said he might want to get involved in the local life underwriter organization and do speaking and writing to share the expertise of his very successful career. I knew his wife, who was a very intelligent woman with the instincts of our profession and suggested it wouldn't be a bad idea to somehow involve her in the business. The cure I recommended for his menopause was only do those things he enjoyed doing. I suggested he schedule multiple vacations during the year and frequently take three-day weekends. Down time is great therapy for a bored workaholic.

I got a very nice thank you letter from him after our visit, but didn't hear what he was doing about my suggestions for about a year. When I did see him, I got a big hug, and he told me he just completed the best year of his entire career. His production reached an all-time high, he took more time off than he had ever done in his life, and he was enjoying every minute. His wife had gotten licensed and was part of his office organization, and he did find an aspirant in the agency he was associated with who had taken over all of the unpleasant client relationships.

In the start of most of our careers, if we are going to succeed, we do what we have to do. When we've reached the level of competence and success we aspired to achieve, we should slowly evolve to only do the things we want to do, not all the things we have to do.

That said, I think a caution is appropriate. I once had one of my better agents describe his work week to the entire agency. It was an interesting system. When he worked, he was a workaholic. Every Monday he would get on the phone and not stop calling until he had appointments scheduled every half hour for the following day. He nest prospected in corporations; many of his prospects were all in one building and a half hour interval was adequate. So, on Tuesday he would see as many as 16 people in formal interviews. Wednesday he returned to the phone, booking all day Thursday. Friday was in effect his day to do whatever he wanted to do – haircuts, golf, you name it. He had an assistant that did most of the paperwork and it was an interesting, but for him, very effective weekly schedule. After sharing his work week, I let several weeks pass and at a meeting of our relatively new and somewhat less effective associates, asked what they had learned from his presentation, and what they had changed in their operation. I was surprised to learn the common denominator for most of them was they were taking Friday off. They didn't make dozens and dozens of phone calls every Monday and Wednesday, and they didn't have over 30 interviews a week, but they did take the time off.

The reason I share that story is the reader might hear the plan that changed the life of my friend with menopause and pick out only the good parts. Unless you have a very large clientele with lots of A and B clients, and unless you have the skill and knowledge to effectively provide that quality prospect and client with the proper financial advice, the fun parts of the menopause solution are likely to be premature. However, a dream for the future is worth chasing, and as I have already suggested, during the early career, do what you have to do; once you have earned the right, do what you want to do.

Chapter 13

TIME EFFICIENCY

All of the timeless techniques already described in this book notwithstanding, many practitioners find it difficult to effectively and productively utilize their time. As a result, they see too few people and spend too much time doing service work for the people they do see. To be a super achiever, the practitioner must learn to be time effective. Every human being begins each year with exactly the same amount of time. Learning to utilize that time with systems and procedures is one component of every successful person's daily living.

For the financial advisor, the first step is to divide one's activities into compartments. Every compartment in a practitioner's life deserves specific allocation of time and specific attention. Certainly, a high priority compartment would be family. Family time is essential and should be scheduled into every week and religiously adhered to. The business compartment also requires specific time. The number of weeks allocated for business during the year is a variable based on the practitioner's needs and desires.

Down time and recreation time for the advisor's physical and mental well being is also essential and should be scheduled into every week. There should be off days, long weekends and week long vacations built into the annual schedule. Volunteer work, in and out of the industry, requires a certain amount of time and should be allocated and rigidly enforced.

In my early years I worked a 52 week year and only took time off on occasional weekends. With the passage of time, I found I could achieve my business objectives by reducing the number of work weeks, and in my more recent mature decades, I only worked a 40 week year.

One of the systems I used to keep control of my time efficiency was in October of every year, I did a planning session for the entire following year. At that time I determined how much time to allocate to each of the compartments: family, work, recreation and wellness, and volunteerism. I pre-scheduled family time into every week and allocated specific weeks for work and specific weeks for rest and relaxation. I began a calendar for the following year, where I entered all special occasions for the family, as well as the major meetings I knew I planned on attending, both for business and community purposes. I penciled in all client reviews on specific days, realizing that they might not be available for those specific days, so there was some built in flexibility if I had to make changes. I tried to pre-schedule for the entire year, every breakfast and lunch three to four days a week, leaving the unscheduled days for my assistant to reschedule where the client or business associate was not available. I entered all of the recreational activities for which I had pre-purchased tickets in blocks of six and used those occasions to pre-schedule invitations to my A and B clients, as well as my most important friends, family, and business associates.

The days I allocated for work anticipated a minimum of a 12 hour day, which even with only a 40 week year, gave me more working hours than many people have working a 52 week year. At the same time, I figured out what my production objectives were for the year, and once that number was determined, I divided the number of work weeks (in my case 40) into those objectives to determine my work week goals. Of course, the calendar had to be adjusted during the year. My assistant received a duplicate copy with all the appointments that were pre-scheduled, but which the client was unaware. My assistant would call the client a week or two in advance to actually firm up the appointment or find another mutually acceptable time. I personally made the phone calls for the theater and ballgame type invitations, which were purely social.

For this system to work, it must be rigidly embraced with discipline and record keeping accountability. It also anticipates prioritizing one's activity for each individual day. It has been my belief that 7:00 a.m. to 7:00 p.m. is an advisor's prime time. The media, television, and radio have prime time schedules in the evening when people are likely to utilize their services. Since the only thing an advisor does for which he or she is paid is people related, prime time for the advisor should mean using every moment from 7:00 a.m. to 7:00 p.m. to be with, or talk to, people. Paperwork should either be delegated or done in non-prime time hours. If the advisor's goal is to see at least 15 people a week, the priority for every working day is first to fulfill your people objectives before doing any other kind of work. I actually saw more than 15 people every week and that was achieved by having breakfast and lunch pre-scheduled each week, for at least four days. That priority gave me eight or 10 people contacts without using any normal appointment time. I generally had one or two dinner engagements, often social, and frequently involving theater or some social event. It was not unusual for me to have 12 people contacts before a week began and before a single morning or afternoon appointment was scheduled.

People contacts represent a much broader audience than just potential clients. They include non-interviews, sessions with my staff, community activities, existing client reviews, telephone visits with key people, but from 7:00 a.m. to 7:00 p.m., including all breakfasts, lunches, and some dinners, every possible minute was spent with, or communicating with, someone. Rarely was there completely empty time when there was no one to see. When that did occur, rather than reverting to paper

> Paperwork should either be delegated or done in non-prime time hours.

and computers I would go to where there was a good chance of being with people, perhaps just doing non-interviews. As a manager, every single day, often with a can of soda in my hand, I would walk around the office and visit each of the associates, staff, management, and sales associates. These walk-arounds were not just to say hello, but to stop and really talk to each of them individually. Often, using the principle of listening with your eyes and your heart, I could tell when they had a problem, which they did not verbalize. I would use that opportunity to have a more intimate and personal discussion.

Since the successful whole person has compartments other than work related, the same type of prioritizing and discipline should be utilized on the days and weeks allocated to those compartments. Family time presumes personal time with family members, as well as a lot of normal participation in the recreational activities of children and spouse.

Volunteerism has to be controlled. Some people become almost full time professional volunteers. I commend their intent, but it can get out of hand and be counter productive. Certainly built in to every practitioner's life there should be ample time for volunteer business and philanthropic and community type activities. Also, accepting chairmanships and officer positions in those organizations is to be encouraged. However, the amount of time allocated to those activities cannot negatively impact any of the other compartments. Business and family time is sacred. Being active in many organizations and activities is appropriate. However, accepting responsibility for leadership that requires additional time must be rationed. In most cases, one can really effectively address only one organization at that level at any one particular time.

Recreation and well being deserves part of every day. Working out every morning or evening is essential for good health. Down time, such as vacations, three-day weekends, days for just catching up should be built into every advisor's schedule. To be completely sharp and at one's best, you cannot burn the candle at both ends. Your body and your mind deserve periodic recharging.

One of the advantages of doing a calendar a year in advance and scheduling all these activities is that, in effect, time is being rationed and allowed for each activity. It is unlikely, if you stick to the pre-arranged schedule and only adjust it when conflicts arise, you will cheat on any of the priority compartments by changing time allocations.

With this overview as the background, there are many specific things that can be done to maximize our time efficiency. The question is what methods are right for you. There appear to be two totally different types of people who both master the effective use of time; but, in effect, they have to do it their way.

One of my best friends, who is no longer with us, was Frank Sullivan. When he became president of the Million Dollar Round Table he was the youngest person ever to achieve that distinction. He had many great talents, and time control was certainly one of his greatest strengths. He used every moment and had extraordinary talent in maintaining relationships with everyone he ever met. If he just passed you in the hallway, you might get a note the next day, handwritten, always in green ink, acknowledging the brief contact and indicating that he hoped there would be another opportunity for a more intimate visit in the future.

He had systems for absolutely everything. One year, he and I were attending a major insurance meeting and we shared a suite. One evening, the two of us relaxing in our suite, talked about many things and I asked this question: "Frank, how are you so fantastically time efficient and still do such a fantastic job of production and business and interpersonal relationship activities?" I told him I had never seen anyone as organized and as disciplined, down to the smallest detail, and I couldn't begin to do the things he does his way. He laughed, and then shocked me with his answer. He said, "Norman, I have admired your efficiency and wish I could do it your way. I need systems and procedures, or I would drop the ball. I've learned the discipline of watching the clock, keeping records, making notes, and communicating with phone and written messages in order to get the job done. You don't do any of that and still you get the job done; I wish I could do it your way."

At the conclusion of an extended visit on that subject, we realized there are some people who have developed "seat of the pants" techniques (and I guess that is me) that work. They have a personality and built-in control system that make it work. There are others where time control doesn't come naturally and being efficient and organized requires systems and procedures. The only way they can reach their maximum effectiveness is by installing and implementing very precise systems. Frank was Frank, and Norman was Norman, and we both apparently found effectiveness, but we were doing it two totally different ways. The message for the reader is that your personality type doesn't matter, you must find a way to be organized, disciplined, and effective. You must prioritize your life so you get the important things done, either with precise systems or built-in discipline instincts. Some of the more instinctive approaches that I utilize are worth sharing and, if appropriate, can be embraced by the reader.

Delegation is one of the most important attributes of either personality type. A good analogy would be the new car/automobile sales business. Every customer has learned that when they are considering purchasing a new automobile, they will visit several automobile showrooms and spend time with the sales people. Eventually, they will decide which car they want to buy and from which dealer, and they will make the purchase. They may occasionally go back to the showroom to visit their salesperson. However, from the point of purchase on, if there were any problems with the car that require service or repairs, they drive to the same dealer, but into the service area to visit the service people. They don't even think about visiting the salesperson about service. The most effective financial advisors have similar relationships with their clients. The people contact, the annual reviews, and the sales situations are never delegated and

Delegation is one of the most important attributes of either personality type.

are conducted by the practitioner. However, almost all the paperwork and routine service and administrative functions are conducted by staff. In many cases, the client gets to know the staff person almost as well as they know the advisor. The client also knows that by going to the staff person, they can probably get service work done more quickly. Every job function that can be done by a lower paid individual, rather than the high paid advisor, ought to be delegated. If 7:00 a.m. to 7:00 p.m. is people time, most of the paperwork and administration must be done by somebody else.

One of the advisors I coached was a very ordinary achiever when we started our relationship. He had no staff and was doing every part of the job function himself. I recognized his great potential, and though his income was modest, convinced him to hire a staff person and spend all of his time with people who were potential or existing clients. That year he did as I suggested and hired an individual and his production doubled. This didn't happen simply because he hired an assistant but rather because he used the time that the assistant liberated for him to see more people. An assistant will not increase one's production if the advisor doesn't increase his or her activity concurrently. My protégé now has six assistants and is producing at significantly more than top of the table levels of production. His gross income is in excess of $1 million dollars per year and even with six assistants his net income is way beyond his original dreams and expectations.

Even with proper delegation there is still paperwork that must be done by the practitioner. In my case, all of my compartments were filled to overflowing, family time was sacred, business was cut down to 40 weeks a year, volunteerism in and out of the industry was a significant part of my life, which included writing books and speaking, and 12 weeks a year was used for family, recreation and well being, and the non-working business compartments. Despite all of the above, I could do all of my paperwork in two sessions per week. I chose to clear two nights every week specifically for paperwork. Since 7:00 a.m. to 7:00 p.m. was prime time, I began the paperwork around 7:00 p.m. There were times when I was finished by 10:00 p.m., and I will admit on rare occasions I worked until 1:00 a.m. I never stopped until every last piece of paper had been addressed. At the end of every paper session, my desk was clear down to the bare wood, with nothing stacked on the window sills or hidden away somewhere in the office.

That required a second system, which took a while to learn. Never touch the same piece of paper twice. All my mail and phone messages, all the paperwork, applications, and proposals were deferred to those two night sessions. The pile would be pretty high, but I would start with the top piece of paper first. I would never sort through the pile for the "good stuff" but took the paper, one piece at a time, and completed whatever had to be done, immediately. I dictated where dictation was necessary or buck slipped it over to somebody else in the office, if it could be delegated. If I didn't think it deserved my attention, more often than not, I trashed it. The only exception was magazines and periodicals, which I wanted to read. In that case, I would drop them into my open attaché case at the foot of my desk. I would carry those magazines

Never touch the same piece of paper twice.

with me until I had a chance to read them or the next issue came. If the next issue arrived before I had read the preceding issue, I threw the previous issue out. If there was ever an article I subsequently heard about and wanted to read, somebody in the office who was a pack rat had them stacked up and available. I did not accumulate back issues.

I kept a "things to do today" list with all the phone calls that have to be made. I had the home numbers of most of my important clients and contacts available, so that I could call them in the evening when I was doing the paperwork. If I couldn't reach them, I put them on my "things to do today" list and called them during dead time the next day. They counted as appropriate activity during people prime time.

Checks and bills were bucked over to my bookkeeper by yellow stickies. If I had to get up and go to the file, or do some research to complete a transaction that could not be delegated, I did it right on the spot. In the quiet evenings, without phone or people interruptions, it's amazing how much you can get done in a relatively short period of time.

With modern technology and cell phones, and blue tooth in the car, telephoning during the day, which had previously been dead travel time, suddenly became very valuable. Dictating equipment, small enough to fit into your pocket, also made recording information after an interview very simple. I did not have a computer on my desk, though I have one at home. I preferred not to spend time in the office on the computer. All of my staff had computers, so I could request whatever information I needed and have it almost immediately. On rare occasions, I would go to an office computer and do it myself.

Bookkeeping is not one of my favorite jobs, and as I suggested in the Frank Sullivan story, I hate systems and procedures, so I learned to depend on plastic. I have always had two or more credit cards for my personal use and two or more credit cards for business purposes. I keep a detailed diary of everything I'm doing and my assistant has a duplicate. Every appointment is recorded and my assistant knows where I am all the time. At the end of every day, I take the credit card slips that I have accumulated and give them to my assistant. The assistant can tell by which credit card was used, whether it was a personal or business expense. If it was a business expense, it can be cross indexed with my diary to determine who I had lunch or dinner with and where we met. I try to remember cash expenditures that are business related, like taxi cabs and tips, and tell my assistant about them, but admit, on occasion, those fall through the cracks. I prefer to lose a few dollars of tax deductibility than keep more precise records. This system works for me. The precise systems worked for Frank Sullivan.

Having been an agency manager and a coach, I have watched hundreds of other practitioners, and I am amazed at the amount of time many of them spend sitting in their office playing prospect solitaire, doodling on the computer, moving paper from one side of the desk to another, or stacking it on the floor or the window ledge. Some of them are reasonably good producers, but few, if any, are great. Time is money and seeing people is the only way a financial advisor gets paid. It doesn't matter if it is fee or commission based; there is a direct correlation between the advisor seeing people and their own income and productivity.

If there were a road map for a typical advisor to follow, it might go sequentially as follows: What is the appropriate personality type system for you? Do you need precise time control systems and procedures to be effective, or do you have the natural instincts to be time efficient? Either way, presume you must put into place some overall procedure to achieve your personal goals. Budgeting time is as important as budgeting money.

Compartmentalizing your life would be the next step. How much time at your current stage of development must you devote to your business? Regardless of that answer, schedule family time, time for your own recreation and well being, and what level of volunteerism is appropriate. For the relatively new practitioner, work time would have to be quite extensive, which would mean limited time for the other compartments, but family time must be built in. I have seen too much marital stress and resentful children come from the families of workaholics in the insurance and financial service business that can be easily controlled with time allocation.

The next step, from a business perspective, is to set goals for the year and divide those goals by the number of weeks assigned to the work compartment. Rigidly, through accountability, achieve those weekly goals. This requires prioritizing which activities take precedence over others. With or without a staff, the first priority has to be seeing enough people, and everything else must yield to that priority. Finally, the goals should be established before a year begins and reviewed periodically during the year to see if adjustments are necessary. The only way to effectively analyze the advisor's performance is to keep accurate records of activity and productivity and based on hard facts, then make the necessary adjustments at each review. There are only two ways to improve productivity, and they are to either make more sales or make bigger sales. Geometric growth can only come from doing both concurrently. When the goal and result reviews, which should be done on at least a quarterly basis, are analyzed and compared with the annual objectives, adjustments would either require more activity or more effective skill levels to increase the average size of the individual plans, or a combination of the two.

For many years I used the expression that "this is a very easy business," because a practitioner can learn to be a successful advisor in a matter of months. It is not like medicine or rocket science, which takes many years to learn. One day, I was speaking to a group of reasonably successful practitioners and I used the expression, "this is a very easy business." One of the attendees, who was also a very good friend, jumped up and said, "Norman stop saying this is an easy business. You are right, it is something you can learn in months, and you don't have to be a rocket scientist or a physician to practice, but you are using the wrong word. It is not an 'easy business,' it is a 'simple business.'" I learned something that day because he was absolutely right. This is a simple business, but it is definitely not easy. To master the skills, the timeless techniques, and the knowledge that is required, and combine it all into one individual advisor's very being, is truly a challenge. However, with a combination of desire and discipline, an individual can lead an extraordinary life, while concurrently becoming a master financial advisor.

Chapter 14

PEOPLE RELATIONSHIPS

How do you define happiness? Certainly a significant part would be an individual's self-esteem, which may be a bi-product of success as they perceive it. Most of this book has attempted to get the reader to enjoy success and self-esteem. The second part of happiness is a direct reflection of good interrelationships with people. Therefore, in the simplest form, happiness can be defined as enjoying self-esteem and having great interpersonal relationships with lots of people. One gets a warm cuddly feeling thinking back to all the lives they have touched who today are enjoying a better life because of the relationship. Most individuals also feel a great love and affection for people, who contributed to their own well being. We have discussed people relationships, particularly in Chapter 9 (Seeing People), from a business perspective. There are, however, multiple kinds of interrelationships, both business and social, that have little or nothing to do with producing sales and income. In many ways, those types of relationships represent a more valuable benefit than the commission dollars or fees they might represent. Along with self-esteem, they contribute mightily to most people's happiness. The people we individually help and the people who have helped us – family, friends, and business associates – all help to make life worth living and will also contribute to our business success. We will discuss many categories of relationships in this chapter, but let's begin with the most important one, family.

Parents, the spouse, and children are certainly the first priority for most people. The Million Dollar Round Table has aggressively promoted the concept of family time, which emphasizes that the family compartment in each business person's life is the highest priority. My wife, Sandy, and I recognized that truth before The Round Table started their family time program. Regular and intimate relationships with our parents and time devoted to each other and our children have always been the first priority in our life. In our case, while our children were still very young, we decided that besides the frequent visits with family members, we would like to devote a special time every year just for our immediate family. We realized in time the children would grow, develop new and important interests, marry, and have children of their own. We wanted to establish a tradition that would supersede all other activities for the rest of our lives. We decided to call that special annual gathering the Levine Outing, and this year we enjoyed our 38th consecutive year of these annual visitations. As an example, this year Sandy and I hosted a cruise restricted to that immediate family, which now includes our children, their spouses, and their children. No one else is allowed to be with us on these annual occasions. No eligible family member has ever missed attending a Levine Outing. Though we see the entire family many times during the year, particularly holidays and special occasions, the Levine Outing is very special. We've been to Hawaii, Florida, and lots of places in between. This year was our third Levine outing cruise. On occasion we've had a quieter visit closer to home, but always private, just for the immediate family, and hosted by Sandy and me. We have found that it is a wonderful way to maintain a close relationship with the evolving, expanded family, and by beginning it when the children were very young and still living at home, the tradition was well established before other significant interpersonal relationships developed as the children matured.

A question I am often asked by people in the financial service business is how can they get their children to follow in their footsteps and become financial practitioners? Often that is because the children resent the intense work ethic of their parents and blame the business for not having a closer relationship with the family. We have three children, and they are all in the financial service business, though I never asked them to become financial service professionals. Initially, they were all part of my organization until I retired as a manager, but that was their choice. By carving out significant family time, none of the resentment that some of my friends have experienced ever occurred, but there is another thing that we have done that might have contributed to the children making the career decisions they chose to make. We made sure our children knew what we were doing and why we were doing it. They understood helping people face the three inevitable risks already discussed in this book. When they were not required to be in school, they were with us at all company and business meetings, even when family attendance was discouraged. When necessary, they would stay nearby with Sandy, and either pre- or post-meeting, we'd all get together and piggyback some fun family time. When possible, they attended meetings and heard the speakers and met our friends. Our son, Dan, chose to give up a medical career and become an insurance person because he concluded the nicest people he ever met were our friends in the insurance business. Our daughter, Linda, studied to be a school teacher, but when she matured, she decided to work in the financial service industry and joined my organization. Our son, Don, became a businessman after college, working for major corporations, but then decided he would rather be an entrepreneur and build his own business in the financial service industry and asked if he could join our organization. None of them were encouraged to be in our business. All three of them chose to be in our business because of the lifestyle and the people they enjoyed due to our family time relationships. Sandy and I believe our family is our number one achievement, and the most wonderful part of our life. The frequent presence of family and the road they have each chosen to travel is surely a reflection of our great intra-family interrelationships. Another piece of evidence regarding the success of family time is this year the children suggested they take over the annual Levine outing and host it themselves in the future.

> How can they get their children to follow in their footsteps and become financial practitioners?

Finally, in family interrelationships I have observed many situations where husband and wife grew apart because of the financial service business career. It is not unusual for a recruit entering the business to have good marital relationships with a spouse who usually comes from a similar background. They have lots of mutual friends, similar modest economic advantages, and a comfortable, compatible lifestyle. If the new advisor fully embraces the business, he or she will be spending many hours away from the family. Without providing for a family time compartment that absence unto itself can create stress. By not involving the spouse and children in their business world, an intellectual gap can develop that also creates stress. Presuming success is forthcoming, more affluent economic levels will introduce the practitioner to friends and acquaintances outside of their previously comfortable social world, and once again this can create stress.

Social obligations, which come with economic success and involvement in the community and the industry, also result in interrelationships with people the spouse may not be comfortable with, and once again there is stress. When all of these different stress levels compound, marriages can be in jeopardy. On the other hand, when the spouse is involved and participates in all of these different exciting new challenges, and time is allocated for private family gatherings, instead of stress the results can be increased happiness.

Besides family, friends and acquaintances are very important.

Earlier in the book we discussed the non-interview procedure, which encourages the financial advisor to be a nice person, speaking to lots of nice people every week. We acknowledged that only a small percentage of those people ever become prospects and then clients, which leaves the majority of them as potential acquaintances and friendships. The more people you know who you enjoy being with, even without a business relationship, the happier you are likely to be. You will also have the opportunity, through the influence you enjoy with all of these people, to get things done you might not have been able to do alone. In time some of these acquaintances will become friends and some of the friends will become clients. Though that is not the motive, knowing lots of people is fun and getting their friendship and respect is fantastic. Also, it opens the door to community, professional, and philanthropic activities. Being active in organizations that you enthusiastically embrace will establish large numbers of strong interpersonal relationships, which will last a life time.

Involvement in or out of our profession is time well spent.

As an example, one of the many organizational activities I have enjoyed is when I took my first position in the National Association of Life Underwriters (NALU), now NAIFA, in 1955. Eventually, I went through all the local chairs in New York City, transitioned to the state organization and went through all the chairs of New York State, and finally went through all the chairs and became President of the national organization. My last official officership in that organization was in 1976. For 21 years, I had the pleasure of working on an almost weekly basis with some of the most wonderful people I've ever met in my life, and lifetime friendships were established, which is a priceless fringe benefit. Every volunteer, when they are giving of themselves to a cause they embrace, receive back tenfold through the compensation of strong interpersonal relationships.

It always amazes me that when I need a volunteer for an organization, the marginal and less successful people invariably say no because they cannot afford the time. But the successful people, almost without exception, always say yes. Volunteerism isn't a sacrifice; it is a privilege and learning that fact can help contribute to your personal happiness.

> The marginal and less successful people invariably say no because they cannot afford the time.

Study groups have been an important part of many successful practitioners' lives. I have belonged to three different kinds of study groups. One type was exclusively for people in the company that I represented. There are study groups for sales people and there are study groups for managers. I belonged to both types.

The second kind of study group was regional. My agency was in the San Francisco Bay area, and from among my so-called competitors, we selected those we perceived to be the most successful managers of organizations in our area and formed a study group. We met semi-annually and established great personal relationships that still inter-relate to this day. Outsiders might have thought of us as a group of competitors, but we freely shared our operational procedures and became great friends.

The third type of study group is national, where compatible, comparably successful people from different companies get together, perhaps once a year, and establish a bonded personal relationship.

Having belonged to all three types, but never more than three at any one time, I can attest to what great experiences each has been. I have made friends who have been very significant in my life. I've learned practical best practices from each of the participants of each of the groups, and I have been motivated and inspired by their freely sharing with their fellow study group members. That is one of the hallmarks of a great study group. There are no secrets; everyone freely shares their most intimate thoughts, including company and financial privileged information. The understanding is that the other members of the group will keep that information for their own personal use and never share it with other people. Between meetings, without exception, all the study group members would communicate, particularly if they needed some advice or counsel, which of course, was freely given by their peer group members. When a group is compatible and made up of people with essentially the same objectives in their career, inevitably the entire group grows and prospers, reaching levels that would have never been possible without the study group relationship.

Interestingly, one of the groups I belonged to was the General Agents Symposium (GAS), one of the oldest, most prestigious groups in the industry. All of the members are outstanding practitioners, and all are great friends and an influence in my life.

Phil Richards, one of the members of that group, is one of the people who encouraged me to write this book, which I would never have considered except for good friends recommending I do it. This is just one example of many things that I have done in my career, which were initially influenced by fellow study group members.

So some of the people relationships we have already eluded to – family, non-interview contacts, community, professional involvement activities, and study groups – are constituencies that impact on our daily living and contribute to our happiness. From a business perspective in my personal situation, speaking and writing have opened literally thousands of doors. I have spoken in almost 30 different countries and all 50 states. I now have at the very least good acquaintances, and in some instances great friends, coast to coast in my own country and all over the world.

The heroes and legends I mentioned earlier in this book enjoyed, or are still enjoying, similar exposure to fantastic people, as well as to each other. The 21st century practitioner is missing a great fringe benefit of success in our financial service industry if they are not speaking, writing, and sharing the magic of their expertise. The masses aspiring to achieve need that inspiration and motivation. Obviously, that opportunity is not appropriate for all practitioners. However, for those who have enjoyed success and are capable of communicating from the platform, I strongly encourage them to exploit this exciting challenge. So that it does not become burdensome, I suggest rationing one's time for that sort of activity. In my heaviest involvement year, I spoke over 100 times. But for the past 30 years, I have greatly limited that activity. I have never charged a fee for speaking at one of the professional trade associations that is non-profit in nature. The only exception to that rule was if the association is paying fees to other speakers or insists on a date in conflict with a paid speaking engagement elsewhere. That has only occurred once in my 60 year career, but I do limit the number of these speeches to a maximum of one a month, which is always fulfilled. I do charge fees when companies or profit making organizations are hiring speakers and would like me to participate. I share this information to hopefully influence readers to make themselves available to our professional organizations free of charge, but limited to what comfortably can fit into their schedule.

A major constituency of important people in our lives is our existing clientele. Client service, when done properly, assures the retention of the client and usually, particularly for the A and B clients, results in friendships and strong interpersonal relationships. We have already discussed the contingency day concept with the property book and annual reviews. I've also mentioned that I get six tickets for most things Sandy and I enjoy doing, which means I invite four people to join us multiple times a year for social get-togethers. Recently, I've seen on television a cute commercial by a major life insurance company that takes place at a wedding. The speaker tells how excited he is about the bride, and how he had helped raise her, get her through college, and helped get their new home. The viewer obviously presumes this was the father. The speaker then says, "I don't know why I'm telling you all this, I'm

> A major constituency of important people in our lives is our existing clientele.

just the financial advisor, let me introduce you to the father of the bride." I love that commercial because it is exactly correct. A good financial advisor helps build the dream, puts together a plan to achieve that dream, and then is there at all the happy moments. All financial advisors who have close interpersonal relationships with their clients attend their family weddings, visit their new home, greet the new babies, and reciprocate in kind by inviting many clients to the advisor's special moments. It is not the money we make that measures our success, it is the impact we have on our fellow human beings. The expression that most clients are friends and most friends are clients is exactly correct.

Some years ago there was a wonderfully warm television series entitled "Father Knows Best." All of America watched it and enjoyed it. The father was an insurance man and a fantastic human being. What is interesting is though obviously the show was fiction, the model for the father and the insurance person was a real live human being. Frank Nathan, a New York Life agent in southern California, and a good personal friend, was the model for that show. The writer knew him well and built a complete television series about a wonderful family and community person based on Frank's own life. Frank is gone, but the legacy lives on.

We have covered a lot of constituencies and a lot of life's compartments and the interpersonal relationships that we develop from those experiences. Despite all of the above, as my son, Dan, said, "The nicest best people I have ever met, and who I enjoy as friends, are my peers in the insurance and financial service business." Unfortunately, as I have also implied, the modern generation practitioner is somewhat less giving, caring, and sharing than my generational peers. It need not be so. There are exceptions today, and in the right environment, there can be many more in the future. Before I finish this chapter, let me share a few of the many, many stories of financial service people I've had the privilege of calling friend and their amazing attitudes and contributions. Each was a whole person, but I will only share one example for each person to make the point. I'm not doing this in any special order, but at random, and I am only barely scratching the surface in doing so.

First, the late and wonderful John Savage. At the University of Toledo there is a Savage Hall. At both the University and his church, they prominently recognize his lifetime of contributions. At his home he had multiple basketball courts in the backyard where he entertained inner city youth, and he gave them all gifts of basketball shoes and equipment. Typical of his giving attitude, here is just one story about the great super producer from Toledo, Ohio.

I was speaking in Alabama at a sales congress. The night before the congress, we learned that one of the key advisor speakers, who was also a gentlemen farmer as a hobby, had turned his tractor over, been pinned underneath, and had a broken leg. Fortunately he would survive, but he was taken to the hospital and obviously was not going to be able to speak. We learned this at dinner the night before the sales congress, and the committee chairman wanted a major speaker and thought it would be great if they could get John Savage. They knew he was a close personal friend of mine and asked me if I thought he would come. I said, "Frankly, I doubt it." It was late to even extend an invitation, let alone expect him to travel all night to get there, but they insisted I at least call John. I reached John at home that night and explained the situation. He said let me check the air travel connections and I'll call you back. John took a red-eye and was there for breakfast the next morning. He gave an absolutely fantastic speech, obviously without a fee, just to help out his fellow practitioners. I have probably 20 more comparable stories about John Savage, but I know I could have called 50 other less successful people and all of them would have said no.

The great Lyle Blessman, another 20th century super star, showed extraordinary courage and commitment while serving as the president of the Million Dollar Round Table. On his first international trip as president, he represented MDRT in Australia. Australia's financial service industry was in turmoil. Proselytizing was rampant, and many firms were abandoning insurance and substituting investments.

Lyle and his lovely wife, Connie, were attempting to mediate between the different factions to help find a satisfactory solution. Having achieved all that could be accomplished under the circumstances the Blessman's were leaving and already at the airport when they were contacted with the frightful news that their son had passed away. The worst 22 hours they ever spent was that flight back to Denver. The entire executive group from MDRT flew to Denver to be part of their loving extended family, mourning the Blessman's tragic loss.

Though in shock and severe sadness that lasted well beyond Lyle's term of office, and even though the MDRT executive committee offered to fulfill his obligations until he was ready, Lyle was on a plane soon thereafter to Japan to continue his commitment to the organization and industry he so deeply loved.

Despite the personal anguish, Lyle never missed a beat. As his term of office approached the final days, he arranged for his mother and a few immediate family members to attend the MDRT Annual Meeting to be part of the "End of Term" celebration and to hear his farewell speech.

He had already purchased the air tickets for his mother and looked forward to her sitting in the front row of the meeting, but with only a few days to go, his mom had a stroke and died.

Can you imagine losing a son and mother during what should have been one of the greatest years of your life and still performing like the great leader he had always been? Lyle has always been a caring and sharing leader, with a "what can I do for you attitude."

Lyle ended his year riding a horse onto the main platform stage, dismounted, and delivered a never to be forgotten farewell speech. Only his family and closest friends knew the sadness in his heart.

Gary Sitzmann has a similar story. I invited Gary to speak at a very small life underwriters association meeting in Palm Springs, California. I told him in advance there would only be 20 or 30 people in attendance. Gary had a part-time home in Palm Springs, and it didn't seem like a great inconvenience and he happily accepted. We had scheduled a dinner the night before the meeting with Gary and his wife and Sandy and I. That afternoon my phone rang. It was Gary and he was near his primary home and office in the Oakland/San Francisco Bay Area. He advised me that his father, who had been ill, was now terminal, had gone into a coma, and was hospitalized. I presumed that meant Gary would not be at the meeting, but I was wrong. He said "Norman, I can't make dinner, but I will be there for the meeting and I will speak." I tried to discourage his coming, but he said, "No, I made you a promise, I'll be there."

The next day Gary had arranged for a private jet, at his expense, to fly to Palm Springs first thing in the morning. The jet waited on the tarmac of the airport while Gary took a taxi to the meeting site and at one o'clock sharp started his speech. Between 1:00 p.m. and 1:05 p.m. he was talking about his father and what a great influence and mentor he had been and that his dad was lying in a coma in the hospital. He then said he knew that if his dad had been alert, he would have told him what he had always taught him, a commitment is a commitment, "Gary, you've got to go to the meeting." He finished talking about his dad at 1:05 p.m. and went on to give a tremendous speech, which motivated everybody in the audience. As soon as the meeting ended, he went back to his plane on the tarmac and flew back to be with his dad. I spoke to Gary the next day and was shocked to learn that his dad had passed away, the day he spoke, at 1:04 p.m., exactly the same time that Gary was speaking to the 30 people in Palm Springs about his father who had made him understand a commitment is a commitment. I have no idea what the plane and the travel expenses cost Gary, but he paid for them himself. Nor do I know what he really felt in his heart, but I am absolutely convinced if he had it to do again, he would do the same thing. That is Gary Sitzmann. He told me he had no regrets and that is typical of Gary. My concern is how we pass that kind of thing onto the next generation.

In recent years, the General Agents and Managers Association (GAMA) has had many outstanding presidents. Two in particular served under extraordinarily stressful conditions: Conk Buckley and Jim Krueger. While each was serving their presidential years, they learned they had potentially terminal cancers. Both had great reason to ask for a leave of absence or to totally resign, but neither did. They both served wonderfully, making great contributions to the organization they embraced. At the end of his term, Jim delivered, while sitting in a chair, an extraordinary presidential address that no one in the audience will ever forget. Sadly, shortly thereafter, we lost Jim Krueger, but in some ways we will never lose him. Everyone who knew him will remember his courage and dedication, his motivation and inspiration despite serving with frightful pain and anguish. Happily, Conk is now a cancer survivor, and after fighting the battle, which he has now won, served admirably and continues to serve as an active volunteer for the organization he loves.

Perhaps the greatest life insurance person in the history of the industry was the unbelievable Ben Feldman. Ben is no longer with us, but he was a pioneer breaking ground that had never before even been considered. At one meeting with thousands of practitioners in the audience, Ben said that in the following year he would write $100 million of new life insurance. That was a number that had never ever been contemplated by anyone else in the industry. He spoke again a year later, after having achieved that extraordinary number. He said, after attaining that fantastic record, that it wasn't that big of a deal. It only amounted to $2 million of insurance a week for 50 weeks. He knew he could do that and he did.

But Ben was very shy. Also, Ben was constantly battling some physical problems that required constant attention. When he first became famous, because of his extraordinary performance, he was too shy to speak to a live audience. He finally, reluctantly, agreed to speak at MDRT provided he didn't have to get on stage in front of the audience. What was finally arranged was Ben was given a microphone and he stayed back stage, invisible to the audience, while a Vice President of the company he represented, New York Life, sat on the stage behind a desk and asked questions. Ben answered on the microphone, but not in view of the audience. It has been said that one of the greatest fears that many people have is public speaking in front of a live audience. Ben's courage at that first speech was a break through session and opened the way for Ben to frequently speak and share with his fellow practitioners all of his masterful and unique methods, skills, and procedures.

Happily, Marvin Feldman, his son, is continuing the tradition among the modern 21st century practitioners by having served as president of the MDRT, Chairman of the Top of the Table, and has been a speaker at many association meetings.

Charlie Flowers was another wonderful friend with a fantastic attitude. He was in constant pain from several painful physical conditions. He wore a butterfly pin in his lapel to illustrate and communicate his love of people. Some of his speeches were built around that butterfly, based on the idea that a butterfly is a beautiful insect, but very fragile. You can kill a butterfly or hurt it easily and in so doing destroy its beauty. He would then make the analogy that people are beautiful, but they are also very vulnerable and fragile, and we should all build our lives being careful not to tear the wings off the butterfly or bruise another human being. He was often asked how he could cope with the pain he lived with every day, also be a great personal producer, and freely share his time by speaking and being involved in the organizations. He responded that he began every day, despite his problems, realizing that he had more blessings than pain. He said that in the shower every morning, he would take the time to thank God for three of his blessings, and he'd think about those good things that would give him the strength to get him through the day, despite the hardships.

I could keep going, but I will just share just one more directly involving a 20th century practitioner legend and my late good friend, Sid Friedman. For those that knew Sid he was always impeccably dressed, had a constant suntan, his hair was always immaculate and perfectly groomed, and his clothing was the best money could buy. He was a perfect example of a highly successful entrepreneur. He looked it and he acted it.

Sometime ago, I was invited to speak at the American College's campus for a Memorial Sales Congress in memory of the great John Savage. There were several of my good friends on that program, one of whom was the outstanding Sid Friedman, and I looked forward to being with them. I hadn't seen Sid for awhile, and when I saw him again he told me he was fighting a cancer that was curable and that everything was under control. He told me that over a period of months, and since he always looked so great and acted so strong, I presumed he was telling me the truth. I fully expected a full recovery. At a dinner the night before the program, all the speakers attended except Sid Friedman. When I asked how come, the host said he had called and was unable to make dinner, but he lived in that general area and would be driving over the next morning for the meeting. I looked forward to having a chance to visit with him and regretted we didn't have time at dinner the night before. The next morning he was not there for breakfast, and the meeting began without him. But he was to speak late morning, so there was no apparent problem. It was a great meeting in the memory of a great man.

Mid-morning the doors in the back of the auditorium opened and I, and just about everyone else in the room, was absolutely shocked because Sid Friedman had arrived in a wheelchair. He had oxygen in his nose, was ashen white, frail and gray, but in a sharp business suit. He was attended by a nurse, a gentlemen pushing the wheelchair, and a small entourage of followers. The meeting continued, so I had no chance to go over and speak to him, and he was to be the next speaker. He was properly introduced and rolled onto the stage in the wheelchair and began by saying that both his doctor and his wife asked that he not attend the meeting, but he had made a commitment and came anyway. He said he loved John Savage and his commitment to John Savage overpowered the directions of his wife and physician. As always, he made a magnificent speech while sitting in a wheelchair with oxygen in his nose, and somehow the old Sid Friedman filled the room with his usual magic. I did get a chance to visit him after his wonderful talk and he said, "Norman, don't worry, I'm going to lick it. As I told you, it's curable and I'm going to beat it," but for the first time I realized it was not to be. Shortly after that meeting Sid Friedman passed away.

I miss the people whose stories I just shared, who are no longer with us, and I will never forget them. I cherish the friendships of those still giving and sharing. However, I can't help wonder how many modern day practitioners would have done what these wonderful people, and so many of their peers, did in these stressful situations. Of course, at one time that was a way of life. All practitioners came into the business and first they took until they succeeded, and then they gave back many times over, regardless of the hardship that each had to face. The first commitment was to return in kind what they had received. Every modern day practitioner also has lots of people in their lives from different compartments and constituencies. Unfortunately, for many, the trend in our great nation since the 60's is to ask the question, "What is in it for me, and I want it now, or yesterday, certainly not in the distant future." Happily there are still some exceptions.

I've mentioned Marv Feldman and Van Mueller as two great current role models, but regrettably they are exceptions, not the rule. I hope, perhaps at least in part because of the words I have already written, some readers will be inclined to mentor new aspirants to speak at meetings, to write their most special secrets, to share and care, and mentor their fellow practitioner to build constituencies of lots of people who will make this a better world.

One thing I have learned from the loss of family members, friends, clients, and business associates, in the end people don't worry about things, they think about people, and it is never too late to start thinking about people.

In that context and as a conclusion of this chapter, let me share what I believe is a great example of the joy of relationships and the vacuum when they are lacking. This story involves another late, but great friend, and his interpersonal relationships. Spence McCarty was a professional insurance practitioner, became president of the New York State Life Underwriters Association and went on to become the State Executive and Lobbyist. Spence was a good friend who I worked with for many years for our common cause. He was one of the New York State leaders who asked me to represent the State at the national level. I respected and admired his judgment. Spence was an only child, and he was married to Barbara, who was also an only child. They married late and never had children of their own. Barbara's mother lived to a ripe old age, so their total family unit consisted of Spence, his wife, and his mother-in-law.

Barbara's mother became weaker as she aged, and Barbara and Spence insisted that she move into their home where they could take care of her. Despite her physical weakening, her mind was sharp and she was a most positive person and a delight to be with. When Barbara's mother reached her mid-90's, it became obvious that she needed regular professional care. Reluctantly, Spence and Barbara arranged for her to be in a wonderful facility that could provide the necessary attention and treatment for her well being. When Barbara's mother approached her 100th birthday, the nurses and attendants at the facility contacted Barbara and told her how much they loved her mother and what a wonderful, positive person she was. They said they would like to do something special for her 100th birthday, but they didn't know what she would really want. They asked if Barbara would find out if there was some kind of gift they could get her as a 100th birthday present.

When Barbara next visited her mother, Barbara said, "Mom, what would you really like as a special gift for your 100th birthday?" After thinking awhile, the mother said, "I would like a baby girl." Barbara was shocked. Her immediate reaction was that her mother's mind had finally failed. When her mother saw Barbara's reaction, she broke into a big smile and said, "No, no dear I'm not losing my mind, let me explain." She said on my 100th birthday I'd like you to find the first baby girl born on my birthday, and then I would like you to go out and buy a gold heart pendant and a gold chain. On one side inscribe my name and my date of birth, and on the other side inscribe the new baby's name and her date of birth. Then I would like for you to bring the baby to me, and let me put the heart on her, commemorating her birth date and acknowledging my 100 years on the same date, but 100 years earlier.

Barbara told that to the nurses and attendants, and said she would provide the pendant if they would find the baby girl and get permission from the parents to fulfill her mother's wishes. Her 100th birthday came, and they did exactly what the mother had asked. As the 100-year-old put the chain around the infant's neck, the room was filled with attendants, nurses, friends, and Barbara and Spence; there wasn't a dry eye in the room. It was a fantastic moment. Barbara's mother died shortly after her 100th birthday, but I cannot think of any example that better illustrates how important people are as compared to everything else. This 100-year-old lady realized her only child had no children and that she was the end of the family chain. Of all the things she could have had on her 100th birthday, she realized what she wanted the most was a link to another human being who in a small way would extend her presence into the distant future.

Each of us, by everything we do, impact other people, each of whom will carry the memory of that interrelationship well beyond a single moment in time and our own lives will be more fulfilled by those people relationships.

Chapter 15

THE FUTURE

Part One of this book discussed the big picture of the financial service industry, including a retrospective look at the last century; an overview of the way things were at the turn of the century, and a consideration of what I believe could and should be.

Part Two, rather than taking a big picture perspective, considered what each and every individual who professes to be a financial advisor can do to become more effective, while still contributing to the well being of our country and our industry.

I am both an optimist and a realist. My optimistic side tells me the future is bright, and we can effectively solve all our problems and leave our children and grandchildren an even better world. My realistic side says that since the 1960's our nation and our industry has been moving at an accelerating pace towards serious, if not catastrophic, problems. It is impossible to accurately predict which way financial advising, and in the bigger picture, our country will go, but I do absolutely believe the jury is still out, the fat lady has not yet sung, and the answer to that question will be the bi-product of the consensus of the modern generation, in and out of the financial service business.

> I am both an optimist and a realist.

In the 1970's, when the United States was approaching its 200th anniversary, I read an article that I have seen several times since attributed to different people. The first time I saw it, it was credited to Abraham Lincoln. In recent years, I have seen it attributed to Arnold Toynbee and also to Alexander Tyler, a Scottish History Professor at the University of Edinburgh, supposedly written in 1787. He was writing about the Athenian Republic, which existed 2,000 years earlier, and he is quoted as saying, "A democracy is always temporary in nature, it simply cannot exist as a permanent form of government. A democracy will continue to exist up until the time that voters discover they can vote themselves generous gifts from the public treasury. From that moment on the majority always votes for the candidate who promises the most benefits from the public treasury with a result that every democracy will finally collapse due to loose fiscal policy, which is always followed by a dictatorship." He went on to say the average age of the world's greatest civilizations from the very beginning of history has been about 200 years.

When I read this, as we approached our nation's 200th anniversary, I incorporated those words in many speeches because he, or whoever wrote it, went on to say, "During those 200 years, those nations always progressed through the following sequence.

1.   From bondage people developed spiritual faith.

2.   From spiritual faith they go on to great courage.

3.   From courage they forge liberty.

4.   From liberty they accumulate abundance.

5.   From abundance rises selfishness.

6.   From selfishness they develop an attitude of complacency.

7.   From complacency inevitably comes apathy.

8.   From apathy people once again become dependent.

9.   From dependence they revert again to bondage.

Whoever originally said these amazing remarks is not important. What is important is that I believe that evolutionary process accurately describes all civilizations and, unfortunately, tracks the history of our great country. It also, in my opinion, though it was not so intended, correctly tracks the financial service and trusted advisor evolution. Both our country and our industry were built on the free enterprise private sector philosophy. Individuals were motivated to not only succeed in their career ambitions, but to contribute to the well being of society and the fiscal responsibility of our country. They freely shared among their peers and gave back, in many instances, far more than they received. Paraphrasing what I have already suggested many times in this book, the 20th century had values and a culture of working together for a common cause and sharing freely of individual skills and expertise. People were running a marathon, not a sprint. They were prepared to earn the right, no matter how long it took, to live with dignity and to provide their children and grandchildren with a better world than they inherited. Today, there are many people who do not have the patience to wait. They want it now, or better yet, yesterday. What's even worse, they often want it without paying the price and are unlikely to share their material goods or their skills or expertise.

As I suggested in Part One of this book, entitlements, or getting something for nothing without paying into the system, are a frightful and growing trend. Politicians are very aware that our entitlement programs are totally under funded and will one day go bankrupt or require substantial additional taxation, or the benefits will have to be significantly cut. All of those options would be unpopular with the voting public, and politicians seem to be more concerned with their own reelection than doing the right thing for our country. The nine steps to bondage would seem to indicate the United States is dangerously close to moving from apathy to dependence, which seems to be a predictor of moving from dependence back into bondage.

Our country, which was built on the concepts of courage and liberty and the free enterprise system, is falling behind in the context of globalization because major population centers, particularly in China and India, are in the early stages of the nine steps, fighting to achieve abundance, and apparently prepared to pay the price to achieve it.

However, as I have already suggested, the jury is still out. I consider the financial service industry the missionaries that have the capacity to rebuild the values of our great nation and teach fiscal responsibility and self-reliance. However, as our nation has moved to apathy and perhaps dependency, so have many financial service companies and institutions lost their sense of direction, as it relates to the mission that created the industry in the first place. Demutualization in the life insurance business, along with the trend in all of the financial services, has shifted from serving the consumer to profitability and self-serving benefits and compensation. Some CEO's of financial service companies make as much money in one year as their predecessors in the last century made in a lifetime. Compliance to protect companies from the litigious world in which we now live has become a stronger influence in company policy than serving the consumer and building individual financial plans.

These trends are good reason for concern about the future and that is the realistic current situation. My generation, the World War II generation, is mature enough so that it is unlikely they will be adversely affected by the current economic trends. My generation's children, the Baby Boomers, will definitely live to see some stressful times, as our society begins to face the reality of the economic situation because of entitlement programs and debt service.

As I said, the jury is out, but there is still time to make the necessary changes to recharge the private sector in the free enterprise system. However, if that is not addressed in a timely way, my generation's grandchildren will pay a very heavy price. The dollar is devaluating, our export/import situation is totally out of balance, our debt service is becoming extraordinary, entitlement programs are exploding, and individual financial plans are being replaced by spend now, borrow for the shortfall, and live beyond one's means. As I write this our local newspaper recently reported that 63 million Americans have no life insurance and millions more have no health insurance. And, if you have $100,000 of accumulated assets, you are considered in the top 10% and wealthy. That's the realistic side. Now let's consider my optimistic side.

> The jury is out, but there is still time to make the necessary changes to recharge the private sector in the free enterprise system.

Financial advisors today are better educated and better prepared to do the good job of helping their clients build a self-sufficient financial plan. They have in their portfolio more diversified products than ever available before, and they are better products at lower prices than ever in history. A typical potential prospect, on average, has more family income than ever before and is at least remotely aware of the inadequacy of government and corporate plans. Competent advisors speaking to the open-minded public are the most obvious solution to reversing the frightful economic projections to which I have already alluded.

I believe this reversal can be accomplished. It begins with improving the skills and techniques of an army of financial advisors, representing all the different financial institutions: banks, investment companies, multi-line insurance companies, and personal life insurance companies. These advisors will need to be missionaries in preaching the miracle of the private sector and the free enterprise system along with consumers building their own financial plan to guarantee security for themselves and those they love. Collectively, that could impact on the big picture at the corporate and government level, but individually it would result in many clients with secured financial plans. Compassion in helping other people achieve their dreams must be the foundation of a good financial practice, which presumes the advisor must primarily be concerned by what he or she can do for someone else.

A wonderful story to illustrate that point concerns my good, but departed, friend, Frank Sullivan. I don't know anyone who gave more to many different constituencies in his personal and business career. His family, clients, friends, business associates, community compatriots, charities, and universities all benefited from his presence. There is a great untold story of giving and love that perfectly illustrates the "what can I do for you" versus "what is in it for me" philosophy.

Frank and Collette Sullivan were close friends of Sandy and I. We worked and played together in businesses, organizations, and social situations. Collette was a perfect mate for Frank, and they mutually shared all their values. Collette was suffering from cancer, and all of us who knew her joined Frank in our concern for her well being. There were times we'd get together and she would be in a wheelchair; other times, when the cancer was in remission, she would walk among us with a big smile and her usual positive attitude. Frank was an extraordinary producer and marketer of financial products. He was a Trustee of the University of Notre Dame, an institution he truly loved. He also lived near Notre Dame and his business was in that same area. After serving as the youngest president in the history of the Million Dollar Round Table, Frank became a symbol of greatness in our industry and an over 100-year-old company, based in New Jersey, enticed him to become president. This wasn't an ego trip. I, and others, discussed accepting that position with Frank, and I know the reason he finally accepted the presidency, though it meant a reduction in income and independence. By being a practitioner president, he could give back to the industry he loved and the people in it. He and Collette moved to New Jersey, where he became a political activist, serving on several volunteer and governmental committees. He was a great president and he and Collette fell in love with the New Jersey home and the community in which they resided. On more than one of our social visits, Collette and Frank told Sandy and I that they were very happy where they were and would spend the rest of their lives, even after retirement, in that world. Collette was physically up and down, but always smiling and always positive, and Frank was duly concerned for her well being.

One day the phone rang in our home and Sandy and I picked up extensions. On the other end were Frank and Collette to share with us that they had discovered Frank was in the early stages of Alzheimer's. They wanted us to know before it became obvious. We were stunned at the news, since Frank was one of the sharpest people we had ever met, and we could not imagine him less than totally effective. Nonetheless, we kept in touch and, unfortunately, slowly became aware of Frank's mental deterioration. Once again, the phone rang, and this time it was just Collette who shared some surprising news. She said she and Frank, in his clearer moments, had decided they ought to move back to the Notre Dame area, where they had friends and relatives, so Frank could be close to his beloved Notre Dame. They wanted us to know that for awhile they would not be reachable because they did not yet know where they were going to live or what their address and phone number would be. Sandy and I worried about them but did not know how to reach them for an extended blackout period. A few months later our phone rang again, but this time it was Frank and Collette's daughter, who said Collette would have wanted her to call us but had preferred to do what she had to do in secrecy. She asked the daughter to call when it was all over. This was the story their daughter shared with us.

Collette, while in New Jersey, had been told her cancer had reactivated and was now terminal. She knew she was going to die, and she knew that Frank was now dependent. In the final two months of her life, Collette flew to South Bend, found a home and purchased it, hired a full-time male nurse, went back to New Jersey, and packed up the house and moved with Frank to South Bend and their new home. She got the house in great shape, had the nurse coming in every day to take care of Frank, and then quietly passed away. She had used her final days, and the last of her energy, to take care of her beloved Frank. This is one of the most beautiful love stories and a story of giving to those you love that I have ever known. Immediately after that phone call, I flew to South Bend and visited with Frank, who at times was lucid, but most of the time not, and took him to dinner on the campus of Notre Dame. Just being with Frank was an experience I will never forget; but then, typical of his reciprocity of caring and love, as we approached dessert, Frank looked at his watch and at that moment, apparently lucid, said "Norman, we really ought to get back, it's getting late and Collette will be worried about me." Even after she had departed this earth and with his Alzheimer's, typical of Frank, he was thinking about people he loved. I took Frank home and the nurse took over. Frank was dressed in his usual green jacket, shook my hand, and then hugged me and I returned home. Frank died shortly thereafter and two wonderful people who had given so much to so many were lost forever. This generation must recapture the giving and sharing, and the values of faith and love, trust, and "what can I do for you," if we are going to effectively be advisors for the modern world.

In 1990, the company I proudly then represented had a meeting where the president and CEO talked about the 1990's being the decade of integrity. He told us that the company was in great shape and the future looked bright. He personally came to me and offered to expand my territory to include two states I had not previously serviced and talked about the great future of our industry and the company. I thought he was a good friend, besides being the head of the company, and totally trusted his remarks. He offered to come to my agency and share these wonderful words with my organizational associates. He came to San Francisco and made a similar speech, waxing enthusiastically about the company, the industry, and the future. Based on this information I opened offices in the two new states, at significant personal expense, and my son, Don, and I left our San Francisco headquarters to visit the new locations on several occasions.

Within two months of that visit the Wall Street Journal carried an article that our company, Mutual Benefit Life, was on the verge of bankruptcy. I contacted my supposed friend, the CEO of the company, and he confirmed the report but said he hoped that a major company would become a white knight and save Mutual Benefit. The rest is history: the white knight never showed up and the company went bankrupt. That was the start of the decade of integrity. I, and all my peers who represented that company, had been lied to for over a year. Once the company failed, it became common knowledge that the executive group was aware of the problem for over a year and chose not to share the situation with the employees, or even with the field managers. The problem came from an over investment in real estate, which in the down market became non-liquid, and the company had immediate demands on cash they did not have available. Interestingly, several other companies were having similar problems at exactly the same time. Equitable Life was a good case in point. Once they realized they had problems, they immediately communicated it truthfully to all of their Equitable associates and suggested that they work together to solve the problem. By being forthright and honest the company rallied and survived, but by lying and attempting to manipulate people, Mutual Benefit crashed. For us to thrive in the future integrity must be universal and truly embraced.

Here is a 20th century example of sharing.

In the last quarter of the 20th century, the financial service industry was under attack by consumer groups on television and the radio. Many outstanding professionals from within the financial service industry responded through the media and reversed the trend. One of the outstanding spokespeople was my good friend, Tom Wolff.

> The financial service industry was under attack by consumer groups on television and the radio.

Tom had started out as a product pusher just like me and evolved, as I did, into a more professional advisor. Early on we shared ideas, and he had developed a concept where on a plain yellow pad he would draw a funnel and then illustrate pouring assets into the funnel with some trickling out at the bottom for the uses in which the planning was intended. Then he would, with a pencil, poke holes in the side of the funnel, which created leakage because of inflation, taxes, etc. It was a brilliant self-created sales concept that in today's world would most likely never be shared with so-called competitors. Tom spoke at Life Underwriter meetings and shared the concept, which was eventually called Financial Need Analysis. He became active in the Life Underwriters Association, eventually becoming the national president, and he spoke all over the world, freely sharing his sales ideas. Tom was one of many; but in today's world he would be a rare individual.

So my optimism is based in part on reestablishment of values and on the financial advisor being a missionary for a return to the free enterprise and private sector concepts. This can be done by financial advisors working together, sharing and caring for a common cause.

Significant parts of this book have been spent on getting to see more people. I've mentioned that the target for the number of interviews per week in the middle of the last century was classically 15 firm appointments. That concept was not extraordinary; it was the rule not the exception. Along with the interview numbers, the target was to sell at least 100 cases a year. That, of course, meant seeing lots of people. One hundred cases a year again was the target and the rule, not the exception.

Another good friend of mine, Johnny Utz, established an amazing record that extended for many years. John decided not to sell two cases a week, but sell at least one case a day. He made the commitment and he delivered. For decades, John sold more than one case a day, year round, and by his example proved it could be done. People like Tom and John were role models for other practitioners and were quite well known because of their volunteerism and availability, and they had a powerful impact on the entire business.

One of my associates, who I recruited as an inexperienced representative, had a fantastic first year in the business. He had lots of friends and relatives, and he sold to many of them to achieve a great first year. Our company invited him to speak at their annual convention, as he was one of the first year superstars. He enthusiastically accepted the invitation. The meeting was to be in September of the following year. Unfortunately, he ran out of close friends and family and his production dropped like a rock. He had no sales for two consecutive months; yet, he was scheduled to speak at the annual convention. I was working with him intensely, trying to get him back on track, and I remembered the John Utz story and shared that it was possible to sell one case a day and once again be a super hero. We made a plan, which together we implemented. It involved prospecting and getting interviews on the 10-3-1 concept and, most particularly, involved an extraordinarily increased work ethic. There was a modest immediate improvement and then again referring to Johnny Utz, I said I bet he could do a sale a day for a month if he wanted to badly enough. Apparently the concept caught fire because he made up his mind to accomplish that target. I admit, even I was surprised because he went one full month with at least one new sale every single day. He developed the courage to call on friends and relatives, even without scheduled interviews, and spent every moment of prime time with people. As they said at the Round Table, if it has ever been done, it is not impossible.

One of the first steps in the nine steps to bondage is the development of courage. A great example from the last century, who is still performing today, is my good friend, Mehdi Fakharzadeh. Mehdi came to the United States from Iran to study at Brigham Young University. As a very young man, he came here alone and landed on the east coast of the United States. He did not speak English and had very little money in his pocket. He did not know how to get from the east coast to Salt Lake, and didn't even know where Utah was located. Eventually, he figured out that he could get there by bus, and with his limited resources, it was the most practical way to travel. He got on the bus for a multi day trip and, without the capacity to speak English, managed to get across the country without having one real meal over a four day period. With his limited finances, he did buy some candy bars to sustain him for the trip. When he got to Brigham Young, he had to take a crash course to learn English, but somehow or other while at college, learned English, met a delightful young lady who he married, graduated with flying colors, and returned to the east coast to begin a new life as an American. He didn't know anybody and certainly was not prepared for the financial service business. Though he was rejected by many potential employers he finally, by first proving he could do it, got a position with Metropolitan Life Insurance Company in the metropolitan area of New York. With nothing but courage, he built an extraordinary practice. Mehdi has led the company many times and is perceived to be one of the great achievers of the financial service business. Like others from that generation, Mehdi to this day speaks all over the world at life underwriter meetings, attends the industry meetings, and is extremely visible. Even in his mid-80's he is still an active, dynamic, exciting practitioner. He is one of the few 20th century stars still producing, still volunteering, still motivating, and still anxious to pass the baton to the next generation. As he often says, "If he can do it, anyone can do it."

> One of the first steps in the nine steps to bondage is the development of courage.

We've visited in this chapter many attributes and values that can be embraced and utilized in the 21st century. Another great one involves loyalty. I have already shared my Mutual Benefit experience, and there is no question that many of the corporate entities in the last few decades have done things that have disenchanted previously dedicated and loyal associates. But loyalty is a great attribute that should be earned and maintained as a two way street in the modern world. One of my great friends, Stan Liss, who regretfully is also gone, was an outstanding practitioner. He was the president of the MDRT and, as a volunteer, spoke worldwide sharing all of his methods and techniques. As he matured and approached possible retirement, his company, New York Life, came to him and asked if he would serve as a liaison between the executive home office and the field associates. It was a job that had never existed in New York Life, or any other company, and would require a great deal of time and a great deal of stress. Functioning between the top executives in the home office and the practitioner in the field meant living in an environment of constant stress. Stan's loyalty to the company was absolute, but he wasn't sure it was a practical position that could serve a good purpose. He discussed it with several friends, myself included, and then had a long visit with New York Life's legend, Ben

Feldman. All of us strongly urged him to accept the position to best serve not only New York Life, but field practitioners everywhere. The company could not have made a better choice. Stan accepted the position and became part of the ex-officio executive committee that ran New York Life and fought many battles, on behalf of the field, with corporate executives and won many of those battles. The mutual respect that Stan brought to the position created a new appreciation for the benefit of home office and the field working together for a common cause. The company displayed their loyalty to Stan and he returned it in kind.

In the area of government and corporate economic responsibility, we have another great current champion – a 21st century practitioner by the name of Van Mueller. Van is a Top of the Table member and speaks at associations as a volunteer all over the country. He is an industry activist and a great modern day practitioner. He is immensely concerned with the solvency of our country and the corporate world. His speeches are motivational and dynamic. They are built on the basic premise that individuals cannot rely on corporate and government plans in the next generation because they are not going to be able to fulfill their promises as they are presently constituted. He also authors, by subscription, a service in which he shares current news clippings from a variety of sources that establish, beyond any reasonable doubt, that his concern for the future economic well being of our country and the corporate free enterprise structure are correct and well founded.

You might ask, based on the negative realities of the modern world, where does my optimistic perception of the future get credibility. I've just shared with you a few examples of values and attributes that prove it can be done. In each instance, I used as an illustration of individuals who are financial advisor practitioners, and who are by their very actions making a positive difference. I've shared stories of the caring and sharing of others, advising instead of product pushing, economic responsibilities, seeing lots of people and reaching the masses, honesty, integrity, and loyalty, and the courage to make things happen. We could have written entire books on each of those value based attributes. I know this great nation, and all the practitioners in the financial service arena, can make the world we leave to our children and grandchildren better than the world we inherited. We must never lose sight of the risk every human being faces – living too long, dying too soon, and the hazards along the way. We must also promote and encourage the free enterprise system and the private sector as the primary source of providing the security and well being for every person on this planet. We must, wherever possible, influence the government and corporate entities to remain fiscally solvent and only deliver what it can afford to deliver to the people that need it. We must concurrently provide self-completing plans for our personal clientele.

One final comment on my enthusiastic optimism applies to the future of the distribution system. It has to exist to get the job done. In the life insurance industry, the career agency system was the backbone of distribution. It was the system that recruited, trained, motivated, and educated new practitioners. Investment institutions, property and casualty companies, and banks, because of convergence, are all now moving in the same direction. Some people are saying the classic life insurance career agency system is dead, but even in today's world I don't believe it; but that is only part of the answer.

Though it is true; there are very few traditional companies recruiting raw recruits for the life insurance industry, it is worth our while to look at the broad picture before we conclude that the agency distribution system is dead or is not being replaced by modern effective alternatives.

First some questions. Is there now, and will there be in the future, a necessary place for life insurance and all the other financial products in everyone's portfolio? Will companies continue to "manufacture" these products for the foreseeable future? Are there more people, making more money, with more complicated financial problems than ever before in history? Is face-to-face skillful selling/advising the only major method of distribution that has proven successful? Will, in time, the proselytized agents and independents who distribute those products erode away and only through recruiting will a distribution system be sustainable? I believe the most obvious answer to all of these questions is "yes."

Now I understand there are problems. Margins are smaller. Recruiting is expensive. Quality recruiting with strong retention is a rare skill and requires significant management training. Compliance and potential litigation requires aggressive diligence. Product competition is intense, etc.

With many companies sitting on a nest of golden eggs, accumulated, in most instances, through the long efforts of the agency system, demutualization has changed the game. Under the primary mutual system, some stock company people incorrectly complained that the field people were overpaid and corporate executives were underpaid. In those days, with just two or three exceptions, it was hard to find a stock company with competitive products and a really top quality agency distribution system. The highly compensated corporate executives and stockholders said they couldn't afford it.

With demutualization, corporate officers have gotten multi-million dollar stock and bonus deals; and the goose that laid those eggs, the agency system, has often been destroyed or at the very least, significantly reduced.

Are those observations clues as to why so many feel the agency system is dead or dying?

Could they be right? Perhaps, but I don't think so. Based on my first set of questions, I believe there is, and for a long time to come will be, a need for our products. Further, eyeball-to-eyeball relationships are the only way they can be successfully distributed.

Happily, even if the executives of the demutualized companies have forgotten our mission and are not consumer, but rather, stock profit motivated, someone always fills economic demand vacuums. And that is, and will continue to be, done within the industry.

Some great life insurance companies are holding their ground. I am proud of New York Life, Northwestern, Guardian, Principal, Mass Mutual, Penn Mutual, Unifi, and Securian, to name a few, for not forgetting their mission.

But a mistake we sometimes make when we discuss those issues is to confuse our traditional heritage with the broader picture of today's real world.

Let us incorporate within our thinking what used to be our property and casualty colleagues, among which are State Farm, Allstate, Farmers, Nationwide, and Farm Bureau. They have multi-thousands of agents with multi-millions of clients, and the companies want them to diversify. In many cases, though they are making great progress, they have not yet effectively learned the "unaware life insurance" sales skills discussed in this book, but they will. In my opinion, when they understand "unaware selling," they can and will excel, significantly filling some of the vacuums.

And how about the fraternals? Thrivent, Woodmen, Modern Woodman, Knights of Columbus, and many more. They reach markets in the millions and again, with upgraded training and motivation, can help fill that vacuum.

The GAMA/MDRT Mentoring Program is a technique that can supplement company programs and result in improved production and retention.

Further, I predict as production from producer groups, independents, brokers, and proselytized agents begins to fall, because there will be too few producers to go around, some companies will put their toe back into the recruiting pond and build their own distribution organization.

If those companies get support, advice, and training from experts in the financial advising arena, I believe that a strong agency type system can be created, even in today's compliance and cost controlled environment.

Also, let us not forget the lurking financial giants in the banking and investment houses. They have the potential of being major players in the future of trusted financial advisor marketing of totally diversified product portfolios if they will sharpen their "unaware" and people skills.

Combine the potential of the committed traditional life companies, the multi-line companies, independents, and producer groups (including the fraternals); project the potential of the banks and the investment firms, and a different pictures appears. Also, if those so-called non-traditional organizations chose to build financial advisor agency systems, with life insurance as a key component of their portfolio, they would be supported by the industry organizations such as NAIFA, GAMA, MDRT, LIMRA, The American College, including LUTC, and so many more.

Again, in my opinion, the agency system or its modern counterpart may be different, but it is not dead and will not die. There are enough people still around with the experience and skills to help pull it off.

With all the values and attributes that have existed in the past as the prologue for the future, the answers to all of our problems already exist. When we add to that formula a distribution system that will incorporate qualified professional advisors, representing what had been traditionally known as life insurance companies, property and casualty companies, the banking institutions, and investment companies, there is no question that not only is the jury out, but there is reason for a not guilty judgment. For the moment, things have never been better, and my optimistic side really anticipates an even greater tomorrow.

Each of us, in our daily living, will impact on our collective future. Much of the book you have just read should be a road map for your personal future. As I told my coaching participants, there are three primary missions if one wants to raise one's sights and be more effective. First, what are you now doing that you shouldn't be doing? Once identified, delegate or eliminate them. Second, what are you not doing that you should be doing? You may have many new ideas from what you just read. And third, what will you be doing in the future that you must practice to do better?

Every financial advisor is more than just a professional practitioner. Each is also a missionary for a safe, secure, and financially sound tomorrow for their family, clients, industry, country, and the new global society.

Facilitating Financial Health

Klontz, Psy. D; Kahler, CFP, Klontz Ph. D

Help clients achieve balanced and healthy financial lives with the new integrated financial planning model presented in this guide. Learn to combine the emotional aspects of finance with exterior financial knowledge and gain an expanded set of tools allowing you to serve your clients more effectively. Available May 2008.

Book

7370000	Promo Price
$74.00	$67.95

Take It to the Next Level
Now Set of 5

Radden, CLU, ChFC

Available in print or on audio CD, this series is divided into 5 manageable topics with scenarios where Cash-Value Life Insurance is often the best solution. Topics include divorce, financial & retirement planning, insurance planning, estate planning, and business & investment planning.

Set

3300000	Promo Price
$58.95	$54.00

Audio CD

3309000	Promo Price
$58.95	$54.00

Shuntich, JD, LLM

The Next Step

An easily readable source telling you why and how to get into advanced markets. Available April 2008
Pub # 2840000
$38.10 . . $34.95

Schwantz

Financial Advisors

Discover proven techniques to distinguish you from your competition.
Pub # 4700000
$38.10 . . $34.95

Arrowood

THE WEDGE

Learn the right approach to setting equitable rates and get paid what you are worth! Available April 2008
Pub # 2870000
$38.10 . . $34.95
